MEMOIRS OF A PSYCHIC MEDIUM

The Gift,

The Wound

& The Healing

Debbie
lots of
love there
xxx

Fiona Stewart-Williams

SILVER BIRCH QUOTE

Everybody in your world has to die. It is part of the law that you cannot live on earth forever. So it is inevitable that the physical body, when it has fulfilled its function, should be severed from the spiritual body and the soul which endowed it with animation. It is thus that the transitional period can be accomplished and the soul go marching on as part of its eternal pilgrimage.

It is of course sad that this happens because many of you, alas, have your spiritual vision restricted so that you see only the material, the shell, the husk, and not the underlying, sublime reality. The eyes of the spirit are open, and knows that the one you love and who loves you has left you physically but not spiritually.

Death has no power to separate those whom love has joined together and made them one in spirit.

Silver Birch, channeled through the mediumship of Maurice Barbanell

Excerpt from the book: Lift Up Your Hearts

DEDICATION

This book is dedicated to all those who thirst for a psychic adventure. Have a love of all that is Spirit. May these humble journal extracts bring hope, encouragement and joy.

In the midst of an emotional storm let my favourite words from my spirit guides reach you:

You must move through the clouds to find that the sky is blue and the sun still shines.

Or when I am feeling frustrated or impatient

You cannot tug a piece of grass and expect it to grow any faster.

Or, when I was younger and single

I am here for your spiritual development not your love life.

Their voice and feelings at times of great distress are always most welcome and for that I am grateful.

For I know that from the world of spirit I am truly loved beyond measure, as are you!

ACKNOWLEDGEMENT

Let me begin by thanking my parents, without whom I would not exist (perhaps I should include God in that statement as well). My mother has always supported my work; thank you. My sisters and brother are those who built my foundation of friendship and love.

I am grateful to those extraordinary spiritual mentors in my life who now reside in spirit for their help, guidance, and wisdom. Please keep it coming!

My husband, who has been on many spiritual adventures with me, and my three children, Jack, James, and Joshua, are no strangers to things that go bump in the night.

I am most grateful for my friendships over the years; some are no longer with us and have ascended to spirit, beautiful souls who have gone above and beyond the realms of friendship. And those whose connections have taught me the most about the human condition in its raw form (the frenemy).

I am most thankful to the spirit world, my guides, helpers, and communicators, who have always held and nurtured me on my path.

PROLOGUE

Dear Reader,

Fiona Stewart-Williams here, and I am a psychic medium. I've been this way since before I realised it had a name. Suffice it to say, I've been working with the Spirit World for a while now.

In my childhood, I played with spirit children, and at bedtime, they would all clamber into the double bed I shared with my twin sister. She was not impressed and asked if my friends could sleep elsewhere as the bed was far too cramped. Personally, I liked the company and the warmth they provided in the winter.

Coming from a long line of intuitive individuals, it is no surprise that my siblings each hold their own special talents. We are incredibly close and protective of one another in a rather ferocious way. I guess that's because we lost a parent so early in life, my brother was only four, my twin and I were not yet 10, and my other sisters, also twins, were 14 years old.

I have kept journals my entire life, writing about things I find fascinating, experiences I've enjoyed or just the plain weird stuff I can't make sense of right away.

I write to read it again, perhaps to enjoy and remember, or to figure out why it happened or what it means.

This book was compiled during the COVID-19 era, though some events occurred years before. It consists of extracts from my private journals. Honest and true accounts of my experiences with spirit and with the living. The good, the bad and the mysteries it provided. Fears that I have encountered and at times still struggle with.

If you are interested in the spirit world, or perhaps you are a developing your psychic self. May my little scribbles make you feel less alone in striving for understanding in a world that at time can be both amazing and terrifying.

I hope that in these pages, you will find answers, direction, or perhaps, encouragement.

With every blessing,

Fiona

TABLE OF CONTENTS

1. REFERENCES

Dear reader,

Throughout my writings I will reference spiritual practices. Some of you reading may wonder what they are and how they operate. So, I feel it prudent to expand on some of the topics so you may find a foundation of understanding for subjects that might otherwise leave you bewildered.

Mediumship Circle is a space to train the novice medium. Circles are led by trained mediums, guided by their spirit guides, to help those in practicum understand their gifts in a safe, supportive, and positive environment. Teaching will be both informative and through practical exercises.

Open circles are usually headed by a medium or someone knowledgeable about all the aspects of mediumship and who has practical experience. In an open circle, you can develop whatever gifts spirit has given you. It doesn't matter if you are a beginner or an experienced medium; an open circle is a safe place where everyone can attune to spirit and develop.

Closed circles are usually by invite only; the people who sit with spirit, week in and week out, can build up special spirit energies and relations by working with the same group of people. Here it is sitting in the same seat at the same time with the same people, and resonance with spirit occurs. It is in these closed circles that dedicated discipline and development take place.

Both circles, open and closed, can be found in spiritualist churches and in the homes of mediums who wish to share their knowledge.

Seance is a meeting of people who are gathered to receive messages from those that have passed over to spirit or to listen to a Spiritualist Medium's discourse with or relay messages from spirit world. In essence, anytime we connect with spirit, for example, at a demonstration of mediumship, technically, that is a seance. A seance can take many forms, i.e., it can be described above as perception mediumship, where information is perceived through the medium's mind and relayed to an individual or individuals. It can be physical when the spirit world knocks or taps with intelligence—not just random noises; there must be a purposeful meaning behind it.

There are tools of the trade, so to speak, when seeking those very special physical phenomena, and one I use regularly is the spirit board.

The **spirit board**, or **talking board**, is a flat board marked with the letters of the alphabet, the numbers 0–9, the words "yes," "no," and occasionally "hello," and "goodbye," along with symbols or graphics to aid the communication. It uses a planchette. This is a small piece of wood or plastic used as a movable indicator to point the letters or symbols and spell out messages during the session.

Those taking part in the seance place their fingers very lightly on the planchette, which is moved about the board to spell out words by the spirit world. I have my own spirit board that glows in the dark, which is very handy.

The Dark. Lighting affects physical phenomena. You may hear me say the "spookie ookies" don't like the light. Indeed, they don't. Light, be it natural or via the trusty light bulb, starts to break down the manifestation of spirit in whatever physical forms it takes. Working in a red light is helpful when seeking physical phenomena or a very low white light. However, I have better results with the old-fashioned red-light bulb when sitting for physical mediumship.

The Aura. All living entities have an energy field. For those with clairvoyant sight, it pulsates and vibrates to various shades of colour. These colours reflect the emotional well-being and health of an individual. It is a vast subject, but it suffices to know that everyone has one.

Trance is a state of altered awareness to attune to the higher vibrations of spirit and its guides, angels, etc. Through the induction of an altered state of consciousness, the medium invites the spirit world to come closer, enabling a more intimate blending with spirit energies. It is a cooperation of both spirit and medium. Whilst in this altered state, the medium allows the spirit being to take control of body and mind to a varying degree for communication, be that in written form or the spoken word.

2. THE COLLEGE OF KNOWLEDGE

Summer 2002

There is one thing I have to say about the industry I work in; it is not all love and light. On the contrary, it is a maze of complex insecurities with dollops of nastiness, jealousy, fear, and greed with an unhealthy appetite to sabotage the good name or workings of another. Just a few of the darker shades of the love that is professed by fellow workers.

I never understood why those who truly work for spirit could be so mean, and yes I have known just how cruel, horrid, unloving they can be. On the way up, I met some beautiful spiritual workers, true to their nature and generous souls. I align myself with those who are more like me and have a willingness to share. For those who had a darker shadow to cast over me, I am grateful for the life lessons I have been taught over the years and the opportunities to grow stronger than I ever knew to be possible.

I cast my mind back to my first ever course taken at Arthur Findlay College. It was an experimental week of trance and physical, and I was rather excited to be going, even though it would be a journey by myself. My husband took time off work to look after our two young sons. I believe James was only a matter of months old when I packed my bags for the trip. I just knew it was going to be a life-changing experience.

The internet was rather new, so booking airline tickets was done via the old-fashioned method of a trusted travel agent. The course had sounded so amazing in the Arthur Finlay College brochure, and on all accounts, it was just what I was looking for. The vibe from the spirit world was a huge YES, so I was very confident I was going to be in for a treat.

I arrived at the college in excellent time and waited at reception whilst accommodations were being sorted. I had booked a single room as directed by the people upstairs. It was a little more expensive, but if they felt my sleep was important enough to be uninterrupted by possible snorers, then the extra cost was of no consequence.

Awaiting at reception was a lady from the south of Ireland, and as luck would have it, we hit it off nicely. Her passion for the physical and trance matched mine. I was no longer on my own; I had a fellow truth seeker on the same path as me.

The course tutor, whom I know to be now in the spirit world, was a rather complex fellow. He was certainly gifted and knowledgeable, but the words of my mentor at the Belfast Spiritualist Church, Marie Pead, were brought into focus on meeting him.

Marie said when this fellow is good, he is very good, but when he is bad, he is horrid! She prayed I would have a good week and bring back knowledge to share with the circle I was sitting in, which, of course, is another story. I'll probably share it with you, but for now, it's all about Arthur Findlay College and what happened next, for it did truly change everything for me.

What is this Arthur Findlay College, I hear you say? Well, by all accounts, it is the Mecca for all those interested in all things spiritual and psychic. This grand property, with deeds that can be traced back to the Magna Carta, is steeped in history, with a significantly high number of beheadings and fires thrown in for good measure, has a rather chequered past. The Stansted Hall that remains was rebuilt in 1871 and incorporated within its structure a small cupola which was made into a bell tower (now situated on the roof of the kitchen wing). Two of the large cupolas from the original towers of Jacobean Hall were also integrated into the rebuild, along with 16th century wood panels and magnificent Adam fireplaces. So, you see, the fabric of the building and the surrounding land hold a relevant place in history.

In 1923, Arthur Findlay and his wife visited the property with a view to purchasing it. They fell in love with the place, and after some bargaining, they bought the estate during the war. It was on loan to the Ministry of Defence to be used as a convalescent hospital by the Red Cross, and it was said that some five thousand or so soldiers recuperated from wounds and illness, some not so fortunate, their injuries being too great. Arthur Findlay had always wished for this building to be a residential college for the training of spiritualist mediums. We are indeed very fortunate that that wish came true.

Countless mediums to date have passed through the great halls, gaining insight and knowledge. The very fabric of the building oozes with the passion of spirit and, of course, those wondering souls drawn by its light. It is, without a doubt, an amazing place.

One needs only to google Arthur Findlay to find the extraordinary man he was, the countless books he wrote, and the college he left as a legacy to all budding spirit workers.

So here I was at the College of Knowledge and I was shown to my room. The complex corridors were too much for my dyslexic mind. The receptionist patiently took me around and drew me a map. She was obviously used to individuals of my making.

My room was at the top of the house, so to speak, just above the kitchen and under the bell tower. I mention this because I was very aware of a little old lady, fragile and kind, who shared the same accommodation as myself for a number of days, albeit in a different time and space. I wasn't fazed by that. If anything, I felt comforted being so way up high, practically in the attic. The only entrance was via the coffin stairs, aptly named for their shape; when you were at the top of the stairs and looked down, the pattern was that of a coffin, used, of course, to lower said coffins down the steep, darkly stained wooden stairs. I must admit, I hated climbing those stairs at night. It just creeped me out.

So, let's start with my room. It was a single, narrow bed with a small, fixed light just above the headboard, operated by a little pull string to switch on and off. The room felt cramped and a little claustrophobic, with a tiny wardrobe and a wooden chair by the window. The window, a small aperture draped with pale green faded curtains, looked out to the top of a tree whose branches dared tip and tap the carefully painted sash windows. If it weren't for the pictures of wildflowers on the wall, it would have reminded you of a cell in a convent. My suitcase, which was of ordinary size I might add, took up most of the room, so unpacking was a must and storage of said case just fitted under the bed. Bathrooms and toilets, of course, were separate and situated down a long corridor with just a few steps past the painting of a monk whose eyes gently gazed at you no matter the angle you stood.

The facilities were most likely shared with other students on that floor. However, I must admit, I never came across anyone (living that is). So, for the week I stayed, the large hospital white enamelled bathtubs and the old-fashioned but functioning toilets were for my exclusive use. All in all, it reminded me of my boarding school days. Victorian and functioning.

All meals were served in the dining room, once you sat down at a table that became your seat for the week. I chose wisely for the group at my table were lovely and all willing to talk about their backgrounds and express their wishes and excitement for the week ahead, as it was we were a mixed group of students, all attending different courses. I knew conversation would flow nicely during mealtimes as to what each student was learning or experiencing.

The course induction was in the sanctuary, a stunning place that looked like a church with stained glass windows and deep blue carpets, a raised platform and a lectern linked to a sound system, quite modern and a stark comparison to my sleeping accommodation.

The course organiser introduced himself (I won't mention names) and his team and discussed the experimental aspect of this special course of Trance and Physical. I was very excited. We were placed in our groups and, as luck would have it, I was in the same group as the lovely Southern Irish girl, Nora, who I had met earlier that day in reception. The first seminar was on trance. There was little from the tutor to explain the ins and outs of it, and I felt a little reluctant to sit as others willingly did. I observed, and to be honest, my instincts were right.

The students, numbering about 15, including myself, all sat in a circle. Nora, my Southern Irish friend, was sitting opposite. I made it clear to the tutor that I would observe during this session and lend my energy quietly. All the students sat motionless for what must have been 30 minutes or so, except for one, Nora. I watched her here as she sat upright in a wooden chair, slowly moving both legs forward. She held them in midair for quite some time before her back and arms swung her around so that the back of the chair no longer housed nor supported her back. It was an acrobatic act that I know to be impossible without being a highly skilled contortionist. It was as if she were being held by an invisible force.

The tutor looked frightened and rushed over to her, placing his hand on her, and straightening her up. The class was over. Nora, bewildered and shocked, came to her senses. What had happened? Nora later disclosed to me that she suffered a massive psychic shock and that countless sessions of healing by other tutors did help, but she still felt unwell and, as she put it, just not right. To be honest, I just didn't feel secure with that tutor, so I moved myself to another group. It wasn't a thing for a student to jump groups, but I did join another from the same course, which sadly was no better.

Experimental for that week was a laptop sitting in a room waiting for the unseen hands of spirit to type, which incidentally didn't happen. The other classes I joined were mental mediumship and message mediumship, not at all what I had expected on the physical and trance courses that had it all going on as per the brochure. So, I took it upon myself to have a word with the course organiser. He did listen to me and told me there and then that I was indeed a great medium and that he would love to see me in his group where he would push me to develop my potential. Delighted with the flattery and an opportunity to grow, I headed back up to my room.

Oh boy, I went to his class the next day as instructed, and he asked me to take the class. You can only imagine how that was received by the other students. Who is she to be teaching me? An unknown! We didn't pay for some Irish woman to share her knowledge. The hostility from the other tutors was most definitely felt by the sneers and angry gazes directed my way.

Though I wished for the ground to open, I did what I was asked. I had, by my own actions, estranged myself from the students, the tutors, and the course organiser. I felt unwelcome, unhappy and without the means to change my flight. I was trapped in a hostile environment and feeling very lonely. The atmosphere of the college changed for me. I was an outcast. Mealtimes were a reprieve from the solitary confinement I had placed myself in, and chatter from the students at the table was a blessing. They obviously knew or felt something was wrong, but refrained from questioning me, as often my eyes would be a little leaky and the odd tear would escape. "Weepy Wednesday," one student said to me in a comforting way. I just nodded and pushed the oven chips around my plate. I avoided students from the course I enrolled in. I didn't want to explain why I was no longer attending the classes, and I certainly wasn't going back to be ridiculed or worse, made an example of by the other tutors. I did attend one lecture; sadly, it was a verbatim of a book I had read on the Indigo Children. This pretty much settled my mind that this course was not for me. Why such a resounding YES from the spirit world that this course would be an excellent experience for growth and knowledge? So far, it had been a disaster, and I started to doubt the spirit team who worked with me.

What was I to do? I had four whole nights before I could go home. I sat in the tiny room looking at the two small pictures of flowers, and a flash of inspiration came to me. I would not waste my time. The healing garden on the grounds was stunning, and the flowers were just beautiful. I had an interest in auras and energy. I would study the plant kingdom, and that's just what I did. At 6am, the dew glistening on the perfectly mowed lawns shone like tiny diamonds as the sun was rising through the morning mist. I saw the figures, some walking quietly in contemplation, others moving to their own rhythm. A hive of activity in stunning surroundings, and it was all happening at the crack of dawn. I made my way to the bench at the healing gardens and began to observe each and every flower. After breakfast, I made my way back to the healing gardens with some pencils and paper to write down what I was observing. After lunch, I made my way back, observing, feeling, and sensing nature. After tea, I returned to the bench that would become my patient tutor, and when it got dark, I returned alone up the wooden coffin stairs to my room, where the little old lady greeted me in silence with a nod of her head as she sat in the wooden chair by the narrow window. Really, was my only friend at the college that week a ghost?!

I climbed into bed, switched on the little overhead bedside light, and looked over the notes I had made. I needed more supplies. A trip to the shop was required. I switched off the light and stared at the midnight blue of the night in my room, untarnished by any other light source, and fell into a deep sleep.

A Change in Colour

I arose early as the birds were chirping, happily going about their business in the tree outside my little window. The shop in the college supplied students with crystals, sweets, and books on every esoteric topic you would have a mind to think about. The shop opening times were planned around courses so just after breakfast and in the afternoon for an hour or so.

I needed to get a few provisions for my own personal study; a bottle of water, a note pad, some colouring pencils, a rubber, and a sharpener, and one clear quartz crystal that took my fancy. I had just paid for my goods and was about to make my way out of the shop when, to my horror, the course organiser appeared in the small, now overcrowded shop.

He started yelling at a Dutch lady, clearly not understanding him. She was about 65 years old with a strong silver plat weaved beautifully and bound with an orange ribbon. She was wearing a shirt with a beautiful fairy motif. She was not in our group and was clearly shaken by the mad outburst. The course organiser then left in a flurry of flapping arms and disappeared. I shook behind a stand that housed postcards of the college. I heard later that day at lunch from the other students at the table that he had taken ill. Others rumoured that he fell victim to the spell of another spirit, purchased easily in the nearby village, but none of those shenanigans mattered to me. I was definitely going to keep out of his way.

Here's the thing: after the second night, after my long day studying the plants, ferns, and trees, the atmosphere in my tiny little room was changing. At first, it was a very subtle midnight blue when all the lights had been turned off. The next night it was more of a deep purple, and by the third night it was magenta. My last night at the college that night was rather remarkable.

The little old lady, as always, greeted me with a nod of her head as she stood by the window, as if looking out for someone. My clothes set out on the chair probably prevented her from sitting, maybe not, I didn't ask her. Normally I would have yelled at seeing an apparition, but her presence gave me reassurance and was rather comforting, and I didn't mind that she was there; after all, it was company. I had climbed into bed and switched off the little night light above my bed as I whispered goodnight to her.

Then, as quick as lightening, or even faster, I flicked the light to flood the room with pale yellow light. To my shock and surprise, a thousand or more tiny brightly coloured lights filled the room. They were different shapes and forms with an iridescent sheen. I panicked. Was I having a stroke? I left the light on for a while and checked my breathing and pulse. After I calmed myself with the light still on, I closed my eyes. Yes, they were still there! I opened my eyes to the dimly lit room and steadied myself, I concluded that whatever it was in my room was a conscious-to-conscious link. For they were there in their brilliance when the lights were turned off and the eyes were open, as well as when the lights were turned on and the eyes were closed. After half an hour or so, I lost my fear. I sat upright with my pillows behind me, ready to fully look and explore and examine this phenomenon. After all, I was here to have an experience, why bottle out now.

I switched off the lights and there they were, stunning bright light energies, all unique. I tried to count them, but there were just too many. It was like looking into a galaxy of starry planets and burning suns. I tried to communicate with them and it was apparent this was not an ordinary spirit kind of thing. Then a thought came to me. I had been observing flowers and plants. Was this their way of observing me?

Were these lights the soul essence of flowers? As quickly as the thoughts were processed through my mind, the lights began to move, as if in acknowledgement of the speculation I had experienced. A vibration around each entity could be seen. Almost like a shimmerin' I tried to drink in the experience. Were they nature sprites or fairies?

Looking at those lights vibrate and pulse to their own rhythm, I tried to memorise the feeling, the shape, form, and depth of the feast of coloured light beings consciously connecting to me.

I awoke to find myself sitting exactly as I had been, with my last image being the shimmering energy around these spectacular-coloured lights. The pillows were still propped up behind me and the bedding looked like it hadn't moved all night.

The sound of the dawn chorus actively busy in the tree outside my window made me acutely aware that time had passed I couldn't account for. I didn't feel tired, no, just excited.

It was the last day at the college. I packed my bags and ensured all my belongings had been packed away and lifted my case down to reception. There was no sign of the little old lady, so I whispered goodbye to the empty room and hoped she had heard me. I used the pay phone just outside of reception and called my husband and told him what had happened. He said, "I totally believe you, but please don't tell anyone because they will think you've gone bonkers."

When talking to the spirit world, evidence can be found, but this was an experience unlike anything that I had seen or felt before. There was no evidence behind it.

I headed to the dining room for breakfast, still coming to terms with what I had seen, what it meant, and for what purpose.

I have never experienced anything like it before or since, and while my first visit to AFC was a mixed bag of emotions, it was the only venue of its kind at the time, so I knew I would return, and yes, with the hope of seeing the beautiful light beings again, which has not yet happened.

I met up with Nora after breakfast. She joined me under a large tree situated near a field where horses were gently cantering and generally behaving playfully with each other. She told me that the tutor in question had been ill and taken to his room for a number of days, and that at a trance demonstration he was told off by the communicating spirit person for his behaviour and that he openly apologised to everyone in attendance.

I couldn't contain my secret. I had to share it, so I told Nora of all I had been doing during my time at the college and the lights in my bedroom. She didn't think I was crazy at all. We formed an immediate bond, and we would meet again at the AFC and in Ireland, where we would demonstrate our mediumship and teach eager groups of spiritually minded people both north and south of the border.

So, I have returned to the college many times, predominantly on teacher training weekends. I mention this because the AFC still holds very fond memories for me. Although I had a rather difficult time, I also had an amazing experience. Perhaps the tutor needed to experience what he experienced and I needed to experience the divine workings of spirit.

I look back at this point of my development as a turning point, for I was introduced to flower sentience a number of weeks after my return from the college and I still work in this fascinating way.

3. FLOWER SENTIENCE

Summer 2002

Marie Pead (now in spirit) the then President of the Belfast Spiritualist Church, the only spiritualist church I might add in the whole of Ireland, told me about the special flower sentience evenings back in the day.

Due to the Fraudulent Mediums Act of 1952, the practice was considered psychometric in nature and thus became a dying art. Psychometry is a psychic ability in which a person can sense or "read" the history of an object by touching it. Such a person can receive impressions from an object by holding it in his/her hands or, alternatively, touching it to the forehead. Such impressions can be perceived as images, sounds, smells, tastes and even emotions.

You see, back in the day, the audience would bring a flower to a demonstration. All the flowers would be placed on a tray. The working medium would select flowers from the tray that they were drawn to, and deliver a message, be it of a psychic nature or spiritually. Of course, on hearing of this wonderful way of working, I felt compelled, nearly driven to revive this art whilst keeping within the law at the time. The spirit world rejoiced, and I, excited and scared, delivered my first flower sentience evening.

The spirit world suggests that if I picked the flower, it could not be deemed psychometric in any form or fashion, and that is just what I did.

My first visit to the florist was to a small shop on a narrow street in Bangor. It had a great selection of flowers. I was drawn to the fragrance of flowers that did compel me to enter the shop. I wasn't sure how it was going to work. I felt the spirit world around me and awaited instruction. It felt like an absolute age. A bucket of yellow roses of twenty or more glowed with interest and a whisper in my ear, "I am here." It had begun.

Seven flowers in total were to be selected. That was what I was told the duration of a demonstration at the divine service would take. Each flower is carefully selected. The flowers reveal themselves slowly, the whispers becoming stronger. As I worked, I listened and watched as the flowers told me about their connection to the great unseen world of Spirit and how eager they were to tell their story of soul survival.

I stood on the platform in the Belfast Spiritualist Church that very Sunday. I was nervous and worried as to how this new type of mediumship would be received. I need not have worried, for it proved successful and each flower was significant to the recipient.

Of course, I have been working in this way for a decade or more, and the way in which the spirit world works with the flowers has evolved so much from that tentative Sunday so many years ago.

The time required has decreased, and the embellishments attached to each flower have become so important to the individual in the spirit world that their story is told in such a unique and awesome way that I am still surprised by the intelligent workings of spirit.

The spirit world wished to bestow a gift that was tangible to their friends and family, a keepsake of their communication. I was only too happy to oblige.

16

4. A TROUBLED CHILD

I am often asked about when I discovered my connection to the spirit world. It's a difficult one to answer, as to when it all began.

I was born in 1966 at the Royal Victoria Hospital in Belfast along with my twin sister. I contracted a chest infection which quickly moved to pneumonia, and it was touch and go for a while. This memory I cannot recall, but my mother, of course, can. I obviously got better, for within six weeks of birth I was shipped off with my family to the West Indies, as my father and mother were missionaries.

My mother told me of the many incidents she had with the spirit in our little house in Aruba.

One of the stories I, of course, could totally relate to. She had been sleeping when my father nudged her awake to say there was a lady standing over her by her bedside. My mother pulled the sheets up over her head and replied to my father that she wasn't going to look and wished to go back to sleep.

It is clear to me now that both my father and mother were aware of the spirit world.

We moved from the idyllic islands of the West Indies to Northern Ireland in the 70's at the height of the troubles. I attended the Fourth

River School in the Shankill Road. The school was moderately sized and flanked by the Forth River, which ran along the back of the school, fenced by a high green metallic mesh.

I was in primary five, about eight years old. The big playground at the back held the chain link fence to the river. I remember all the children rushing to the fence as something was gently bobbing down the river. There was quite a commotion. I stood back from the crowd, for I knew who was in the water. A young man in spirit form stood by me, cold, confused, and very sad, for his body was the something bobbing down the river. My adult self now understands what happened to him, but my 8-year-old self could not fathom nor comprehend the atrocities that this man endured. It is very sad to note that this too was a regular occurrence. I rarely visited that part of the playground as you can now understand.

We, as a family, lived at 3 Ballygomartin Road, just off the Shankill Road in Belfast. This was a particularly known area during the Troubles, one of many flashpoint areas full of explosive tension.

The manse was a huge Victorian detached building owned by the church where my father served. It was a rambling house with a large garden and allotment at the back, enclosed by a wall with shards of green glass cemented on the top. I thought it was pretty. When the sun hit the glass, it made the wall twinkle. It was, of course, a safety measure, but to an 8-year-old it was a sparkling design feature.

The house itself was cold and drafty and rather creepy at times. It was a creaky abode that held its own mysteries; footsteps could often be heard and doors frequently opened all by themselves. The kitchen still held the high Victorian cupboards and a small pantry. From the back kitchen door, it led to a small courtyard built in red brick to the wash house. I never liked the wash house. It freaked me out, so I very rarely made my way to it unless instructed to.

The bedrooms had beautiful large sash windows. Those rooms at the front of the house had tall dark mahogany wardrobes placed in front of them. Yes, it did block out the light and the view we had over Woodvale Park, which was just across the road from the house, another safety measure. Bombs would often be placed near or outside our house, and the windows would be replaced no sooner than they were blown out again. The Troubles in Northern Ireland were like that.

We, as children, rarely went out and the rambling house allowed us to explore our imaginations; hide and seek and other indoor games were played. We were fortunate to have this large house to run about in. The stain glass windows, an original feature, miraculously escaped the blasts and filled me with joy to see the streams of colour dance on the walls and floors during sunny days. The three-tiered stairs were a fabulous experience when sitting on a tray became an indoor slide.

The furniture was sparse and the carpets threadbare. I shared a bedroom with my twin and my older sisters also shared a room. The house was decorated a hundred years ago in the Arts and Crafts Movement. Old oriental patterned carpets with floral faded wallpaper adorned the walls. I can see how this house influenced my love of William Morris and worn Persian rugs.

I was often too afraid to sleep in my room with the constant spirit visitors, so my twin and I would sleep with my older sisters, who didn't mind because they were also aware of the ghostly goings-on. The lack of heating in the house in winter was certainly felt and, on top of blankets, coats were placed to keep us warm. We didn't in those days think we were poor, but we were.

It wasn't all doom and gloom, for my baby brother was born and I remember it quite clearly. My lovely Aunty Alma, heavily pregnant with my cousin Colin, was looking after us as my mother was in the Samaritan Hospital.

It was a frightfully cold December. My siblings and I were watching cartoons in the front lounge when a knock came to the door. I was never allowed to answer the door, but this time I did, urged by my siblings as they were engrossed in the programme.

An English soldier was shouting at me to evacuate the building; there was a bomb; we had to go now! Through the gap of the door chain, this young man screamed at me. I said, "OK," and closed the door and returned to the cartoons. You see, there were always bombs, some went off some didn't and it was nothing knew nor alarming it was normal for those of the time.

The TV channels were limited, and so were the cartoons. This was my time, and I was eager not to miss too much. Of course, my aunty Alma was informed about the bomb by our then neighbour, Mrs. Young (who incidentally didn't look young at all, far from it).

Hands and faces were washed, Sunday coats put on as we left the house; one heavily pregnant woman with five children, her son only two years old at the time. We all held hands as we marched from the house, down the pathway to the street. She was exhausted by the flurry of activity at warp speed factor eight. My aunt leaned against a car that was parked in front of the house to catch her breath. Soldiers were everywhere and screaming at my aunt to "get away from the car." Their use of colourful language offended my church-going aunt, and she gathered us up as the robot winged its way to control the explosion.

We headed off to safety and had chips from the local chippy a real treat for us. We made our way to Sadie Patterson, a friend of both my mother and father who we called Aunty Sadie. She was a historical character and a leader for peace, but to us she was just Aunty Sadie. We watched the explosion on our own TV that night on the news channel. Our windows were boarded up with freezing blasts of wind whistling through the gaps, making it ever more chilling.

Golden nuggets could be found in our garden, and the four of us girls would collect these treasures and show them to our father, only to find that they were not exactly golden and held a more sinister meaning.

Dad, of course, was very busy. The troubles, the pain and anguish of other people's needs came before his family. There could be days that we didn't see him as he tirelessly campaigned for peace and met with families in despair. Many a night, the phone would ring and we would hear the muffled conversions. Or the door would go and the sound of weeping and words of comfort could be heard up the stairs on the main landing where we (all the girls would congregate listening to what we shouldn't be listening to).

My brother was born with jaundice, and we just loved how brown he was. We couldn't wait to tell everyone about our beautiful brown baby boy. As you could imagine, as a white family just back from the West Indies. The news of a new brown baby caused such a stir my mother was very surprised as to the number of parishioners and visitors that came to welcome our brother to the world.

Four years passed from my brother's birth when my father became unwell. My last living memory of him is helping him into his slippers as the ambulance took him to the Royal Victoria Hospital. My mother shipped us all off to my aunt's house, and it was in their garden that I spotted a beautiful yellow-headed daffodil that held my gaze long enough for my father to come to me in spirit form to tell me he had died and was now in heaven. He showed me where he was in the spirit world. It was so bright it hurt my eyes, but I knew it was beautiful. Of course, I told my sisters what I knew, and they were not at all impressed.

My mother confirmed that my father had passed away five hours later. We had all been told that Dad was going for some routine tests. In fact, he was having an exploratory operation and he died on the operating table at the exact time he came to me in spirit form. My mum switched off the life support some hours after and, with a heavy heart, returned to her sister's house to explain to her five children, my brother only four years old, that Dad was no longer with us and, worse, that we would have to move house within two months as the church needed the manse for the new minister.

My life changed in a blink of an eye. It had never been my well-developed imagination that all those visits were dead people and I was now very, very scared, and very, very sad at the loss of my dad.

5. MEDIUMSHIP NOTES FROM ABOVE

23rd February 2014

As I type, my sleeping husband gently snores. It's 5 am Sunday morning, and Spirit urges me to write. I am running a workshop today, and the teaching element of Spirit has already kicked in. Rest In Peace is commonly placed on headstones in graveyards throughout the world. There is a misconception that mediums are disturbing the dead. Yet it is the will of the spirit and the need to convey their important messages to loved ones that bridge the gap between the two worlds, that of the living and those in Spirit.

It is the message that is the all-important focus for those in Spirit.

My many years of training within the Spiritualist National Union focused on getting the communicator (the spirit person) recognised; once established, the message was given.

CERT

Communicator

Evidence

Reason for coming

Tying up loose ends

That was the formula that was taught. Interestingly, the information comes in a different order. First, there is the initial burning desire from spirit to share. The reason for their communication is usually the first feeling that I, as a medium, feel, which can be a myriad of emotions ranging from healing to regret.

We, as human beings, all have the ability to connect to spirit. We have physical senses, which are mimicked by our spiritual senses.

Sight

Smell

Taste

Hearing

Touch

And then there is… Knowing

The first five are self-explanatory; it is the knowing that is the least discussed or acknowledged. It is the sense of just knowing; you cannot back it up with evidence. You just know whether this is right or wrong. It is a delicate feeling usually felt deep in the solar plexus, that gut feeling.

It is that feeling when you walk into a room and get the sense that everyone is talking about you, and not in a good way. Do you know that feeling? Well, that is knowing. And everyone has it—some to a better degree than others.

Often, clients will perceive that you are having these wonderful private conversations with their loved ones. Little do they know the mad ping pong ball game of thoughts, sensations, imagery, tastes, and smells utilised to bring about the communication's fullness. All these emotions and feelings from spirit are sent at the speed of light, so quickly it is true one could miss the importance of that scent or taste at the initial contact.

It is great to have clairvoyance and spiritual sight, and yes, an image can tell you a great deal, especially if the spirit communicator can project that to your mind. Or even better when the medium has both objective and subjective senses.

Objective can be expressed outside the mind, whilst Subjective can be felt inside the mind.

I am fortunate to possess both.

All too quickly, a medium can be caught up on the evidence that the essence of the true communication, the message itself, is diluted. The spirit world wishes to push this emphasis on the importance of the nature of the *why* the spirit is communicating.

I am not a small-framed person; I am rather well-rounded, and in some cultures, they would call me blessed. I like food, what can I say? So quite often, the spirit world would share with me their favourite cakes. I get to taste it, and quite frankly, I am grateful that there are no calories in this instance.

I am not a fan of currants or raisins. I detect the tiny seeds held within, and I cringe a little. Some spirit people share their favourite tipple. Whisky is something that makes me heave. Tea I can tolerate, but coffee is more my liking. Having tried nearly every beverage throughout my life, the spirit world has an excellent database to work with.

It is essential to know that your life experiences in all their totality are used by the spirit world. Your experiences held within your mind and your consciousness is the motherboard of the data at the disposal of the spirit world.

In instances where I have no knowledge, for example, I lack insight, understanding, and experience in sports, I can detect a ball, but really I have no interest, so my database is lacking. Try as I might, I just can't understand it; it bores me enough to stick my head in a cupboard and grab anything with chocolate.

Back to the point.

Sometimes those in life have conversations about the here after, and a code word is established between the two. This code is the what will validate the connection for the sitter.

If the word or code does not exist in the mind of the medium, then that word may not be coming forward.

It is true that the spirit person will do their best to get somewhere close to having access to your memories, but if it is not there, there will be little chance of validating that information.

Whilst it is true that the above formula CERT is an excellent tool in aiding the medium to collate information coherently. It is important not to dismiss any feeling or sensation.

All sensations and feelings from spirit are valid, even though the recipient may not understand them at the time.

Now, this brings me to soul language—a shorthand, so to speak, with spirit.

Everyone's soul language is unique to them and their experiences.

For instance, when I see revolving doors, it means one person has left this world whilst another just joined. Or a pink ribbon may mean breast cancer. Poinsettia means a male child or children in spirit. A very dear friend Elizabeth lost two boys consecutively at Christmas time; their small coffins flanked with the festive red plants etched the pain of loss deeply within my soul. So, you can see how individual the soul language is.

The key to understanding the soul language is understanding and knowing yourself. Mediumship is very reflective, you see.

The essence of this early morning writing with spirit is to remind the student that whilst structure is important. The value in the communication is the *why* they are communicating and the *what* they are trying to convey. It is this very message, this huge desire from Spirit to make contact; therefore, it must be recognised as such. It is, after all, the spirit world that initiates contact. Quite often, the message can be so unique that there is no question as to whom it is from. This is the focus that the spirit world wishes to make the backbone of the workshop on. How interesting.

6. BOUNDARIES KEEP EVERYONE SAFE

16 February 2015

I awoke in a sweaty mess from a horrible dream. It was a battle likened to the civil war, where cannon balls flew willy-nilly overhead with shouts and screams. The smell of stale sulphuric smoke filled my nostrils, and I awoke. I reached for my inhaler but knew I didn't need to take it. My breathing was even and calm, the smell gone. A large Kevin shape beside me slept as always blissfully ignorant of my bad dreams and innocent of rouge smells. I wondered whether his snoring had been assimilated into my nightmare.

I glanced at the clock. It was 4:33 am. I often have prophetic dreams, which would have some bearing on the day's events. I worked out I had at least another 4 hours to sleep before preparing for the workshop, starting at 10:30 am. I already knew of some of the students from previous workshops, but several new learners would be attending.

The workshops started on time. I have a new student who will remain nameless. I see a desire to be helpful and kind within their aura, but there are other colours there too. There was a lack of self-awareness. A desire to self-serve. And to self-sabotage. This individual who could be potentially dangerous by their actions and their words. Yet, in the vast hue of greens within their aura is this immense capacity to love, be loved, and be accepted.

I used the round-robin icebreaker at the start of the workshop. It allows everyone to introduce themselves. A few eyebrows were indeed raised, and eyes rolled at comments made and directed to other learners by this Student.

Everyone must be treated equally and everyone must have equivalent time. So I threw my thoughts to Spirit and asked for their help. For I know the Student will not blend well with the group. For already there were signs of intolerance from other workshop members to their outspoken and off-topic questions.

All students must blend to ensure the optimum results of any form of teaching.

As I sat with the group in meditation, I was made aware of the unique make-up of the Student in question. They had many negative life situations, some brought on by themselves, others taking advantage of the kindness they hold. It was clear that the individual in my class was vulnerable.

Rules and boundaries were the reply from Spirit and a gentle reminder of those requirements to be made at the beginning and the end of every workshop. Something I had yet to do! It would be the next lesson.

The group formulated their rules on boundaries.

Words such as inclusive, kind, confidentiality, tolerant etc. were topic headings.

The learners started to blend, and the teaching sessions commenced with the practical work. All was going well.

Just for a split second, that acrid smell from my dream wafted around my head. I started sniffing myself. Was it me? No, I smelt of Channel No. 5. Just as I should smell. It was a warning.

And then, there it was. My poor wee Student erupted in floods of tears from a statement made by another member. It was loud and it did disrupted the class.

On investigation, as one must do. It was found that during one of the psychic reading exercises, a trauma from their past had been unearthed, which was not letting them move forward. It matters not to what the hurt was. Pain is pain, whether it is imaginary or not.

It took some 45 minutes for the Student to regain their emotions with the majority of the class eager to help. A few of my students who worked in the mental health field stood back; they weren't on duty that day.

Yes, it can be emotional at times during these sessions. The reaction was somewhat extreme. To regain valuable time, I called this emotional regulation Lunch!

My prophetic dream alerted me to a potential situation that could have been made more difficult had I not known that an individual was emotionally unstable. Therefore, rules and boundaries are necessary and will be an essential part of any teaching/workshops.

Occasionally, I get a hit of that acrid smell when I am near vulnerable people it acts like an early warning to tread carefully, cautiously and with empathy.

Update

Unfortunately the Tutor/Student relationship did not survive the storm a number of months later. It was carnage, as the dream had suggested.

7. SO, YOU WANT TO BECOME A MEDIUM

Mediumship is a calling, a vocation. You are called to be in service. When I was developing my mediumship, I was really driven. I had a thirst for knowledge, and I attended every course and workshop I could. I attended the awareness group at the Belfast Spiritualist Church, and within weeks I was in a closed circle. A mere couple of months later, I was demonstrating at the church services, much to the surprise and annoyance of others. Not everyone who seeks the gift is spiritual. It is certainly not all love and light!

My development was rather rapid. After all, I had been connecting with spirit since childhood, so it was clearly not new to me. I had a healthy appetite for all things esoteric. I had mastered palmistry and tarot by the age of 16; self-taught I should add. I read runes in my late teens, and my psychic readings gave me beer money for the weekend. I have always sensed and seen auras and now, over the years, it is second nature to me.

It was in my late 20's that I felt an earnest need to discover what my spiritual talents were. As I mentioned above, I sat in a closed circle for a number of years until there was nothing left to experience, and it was with great sadness that I left. Marie Pead urged me to continue with my spiritual studies, which I did.

I hold awards from the Spiritualist National Union in demonstrating, inspirational speaking, and tutoring. I also hold a recognised teaching qualification. I am also a Reiki/Secheim Master and Teacher. The list goes on.

Everyone possesses the innate capability for spirit communication. We are all spirits first and foremost. I do recognise that I have an exceptional gift that is both a continual and a mutual exploration with my guides. I will never stop learning.

When I look back on my development, I can't say one tutor or another taught me this or that. These tutors and mentors have both guided and encouraged me. That is what makes them great teachers. Essentially it is the spirit world that has taught me.

It is a question that I have asked other mediums of my generation and they say the same. We developed our mediumship via the old method. Discover it by yourself and with the help of your guides and the direction from patient tutors.

The real reason for wanting to develop mediumship is that it is who and what you are, i.e., a medium. Working with the Spirit World will be something you will do each and every day. Now, it is far from butterflies and unicorns, it has its ups and downs. The highs can be very high and the lows can be frighteningly low.

Not all readings are created equal, nor are any demonstrations. What you can be assured of is the support and love from the spirit world. Your client and the audience are another matter. If you are motivated by popularity and fame, a failed reading or demonstration can be hard to swallow. However, each experience is an opportunity to be reflective and open to changing how you work. Managing expectations and educating the novice sitter or audience is key.

The haters and sceptics in this day and age are just as virulent as they were in the dark ages. What have I learned? Don't engage with them. People who are full of pain tend to spill out their nasty things, and what's inside tumbles out. Don't take it personally; it is usually all about them and not about you at all.

As a medium, you are the connective bridge, and as such, from time to time, you may hear and become involved in the most heartbreaking of stories. When everyone has left the office, so to speak, and you are on your own, who heals the healer?

I have, from time to time, witnessed some very distressing scenes and found it hard to process. I ask my spiritual team to intervene. To take away the pain but keep the knowledge so I can help others who are going through the same thing.

As a tutor, I teach the mechanics of mediumship and the fundamentals. I can gaze within the aura and see how the student is responding to the spirit world. I believe it is up to the tutor to help the student realise how they work with spirit, not to mould or create a spiritual clone. Unique talents should be encouraged. I remember working with a lovely lady, Ciara, whose talent when connecting involved scribbling. The drawings and shapes she drew formed part of the message; such a lovely way to work and a keepsake too.

For those who wish to develop their gifts, do so at your own pace. Your enfoldment is unique and will be as it should. Teachers for your development will show up synchronistically. Some will be fabulous tutors, some will not. Remember, everything is a lesson!

It is a beautiful thing to be part of someone's spiritual journey and I have been blessed that the majority of my students are now working mediums and also firm friends.

8. THE DANCE

With one foot in the spirit world and one in the waking physical world the fragile energetic dance begins. I often feel a mixture of nauseous and intense excitement rolled into one a few hours before a demonstration of mediumship which makes eating a meal before a demonstration a complete no no.

No one suspects the crazy spiritual juggling act that is secretly performed with every spiritual connection. No two souls are the same in how they communicate to me. Some are purely visual, others are sentient in that they are sensed, felt. It is interesting that I struggle at times with age. Quite often the spirit communicator will display themselves at a time in which they felt was their earthly best. Others may show me signs of ageing either impressing on my body their pain or by showing me there hands or limbs.

Some of the spiritual information can be received like a film streaming into my head. Others when they draw so close to me I feel their entire spiritual essence and take on their mannerisms, gestures, how they moved, how they spoke. There are times when the spirit communicator hangs back and does not come as forward as I would like. And, no amount of pulling or pushing the spirit energy can bring them any closer. You, see it is always on their terms, the Spirit person initiates the contact.

The voice of a loved ones (the recipient of a message) has a huge impact on the energy I am working with at the time. On hearing the voice the soul will respond either positively or negatively (ie they recognise the voice vibration and are elated and of course the opposite when there is no recognition of the sitter or receivers voice).

Some demonstrations are energetically flat. The audience is mute or worse non responsive. These demonstrations are difficult and require far more of my own personal psychic energy stores to hold the energy. Audiences that are more engaging and responsive create a receptive spiritual energy field and prove far more successful that the later.

Those that are recently bereaved should not attend such an event or private sitting.

It is important that the sitter/receiver reviews their grief state honestly. If you are still deep in the throws of grief? Wishing there were still some way to bring your loved one back? Depressed or angry? Overly tearful or so very sad? If the answer is yes to any of the above a mediumship reading or show will not help you. Grief counselling either in group therapy or privately is what will help you to find some firm or solid ground.

Of course time is not a factor to those in the spirit world in determining if they could come through during a session or show, but having that mediumistic experience before you have had time to process your loss will not be helpful.

It does break my heart when I see individuals so raw with the initial stage of a fresh and devastating grief. Their pain so visible for all to see. The audiences are normally supportive to the individual, however some attendees are not and find the public display of grief uncomfortable, unacceptable or just plain disruptive. Ensuring that the freshly grieving person is met with kindness and supported is essential and that is what I practice. A private consultation with an individual will take place after the show with guidance given.

Some communications from the spirit world are not recognised by the sitter/receiver and that's ok. Over the years I have found that the spirit world truly know their stuff. When a spirit person is not recognised during an event I always ensure that we thank the spirit individual for sharing their information with us. They may not have been claimed by a member of the audience at the time, but 9 times out of 10 I will receive a text or phone call from someone who attended the event claiming the individual as their own.

With so many individuals passing through my mind I very rarely recall my readings or my demonstrations, however there are ones that strike a chord within me and those souls leave a lasting impression. Those communications are the ones I will jot down for they are somehow important. For I believe, we all have something to learn form their communication.

9. HORRIBLE HECKLERS

March 2016

Her thin lips were set in a firm line. Her fleshy chin jutted out in defiance. Arms crossed, she glared at me from the front row. She was a shapely woman in her 40s. Her faded, red-cropped hair made her look more hostile than she probably was. Somewhere in life, she has been brutally bruised; her aura pulsated with colours to that effect. Her pain had never been addressed. It had turned inward and had festered. Sadly, there would be no pleasing that individual, for I have met such people before, and such people can be tricky.

I opened up the demonstration with my usual explanation of how the event would flow. I introduced flower sentience and described how the spirit world communicates through me.

I work with the vibration of love. For spirit communication to take place, I must raise my vibration and the spirit world must lower theirs so there can be a meeting and blending of both energies. Nothing raises the vibration more than being in a state of unconditional love.

It takes a huge amount of focus, passion, belief in oneself, and in spirit to stand in front of an audience for two hours without a script. A tremendous amount of energy is expended during that time. It is an energetic balancing act to keep your audience energised and engaged. Whilst holding and blending with that delicate link with spirit.

It must have been the first message that was given that landed in her sphere. She had been sitting with her sisters. Mum from spirit was coming forward, and she did not like the attention on her sister. And so, the heckling started; she was loud and made sure everyone could hear her as she turned her head to address the audience behind her to say that the evidence provided could be from anyone.

I directly spoke to her and said, "You are the youngest sister, is that right?"

All her sisters nodded in agreement. There are five of you girls present. They acknowledge this information.

I went on to say, "You will not share all the same memories as your sister because you either didn't exist or were too young."

I then invited her to be quiet as I was not directing any information her way. I was speaking with her sister.

I carried on with the message from Spirit. But the heckler had not finished. She stated loudly th t her sister was a simpleton and would accept any information. I needed to be harsher with my reply, and I was both cutting and humorous, which erupted into applause from the audience. What a night, what a night, and it was just the beginning.

I wasn't pleased with myself, far from it, because I knew what I had said wounded her. She became quiet and small.

Perhaps it was the influence of her spirit mother. My heart melted, and I apologised to her publicly. No one should make you feel less than you are. From that moment on, I was back in control of the audience.

The event went swimmingly, with laughter and tears as mothers, daughters, sons, and lovers were reunited.

I am not a harsh person; it isn't in my nature.

The number of people who came up to me at the end of the evening and praised me for handling such a negative disruption should have put my mind at ease. But it didn't.

I was emotionally, mentally, and physically exhausted. This is not normally how I feel after a demonstration. I needed time to reflect on the evening and understand why I felt so terribly low. I did not sleep well.

I ran the event through my mind several times to find fault with myself. I had lowered my vibration. The flash of anger and my cutting remarks came at a cost. I would need to address hecklers differently or just learn to toughen up and ignore such outbursts.

I cast my thoughts to the Spirit World for their advice.

You are aware that individuals in pain can display negative and anti-social behaviour. Be compassionate, be gentle, and, above all, remain loving. Keep your heart space open. Do not let anger steal the joy it is to be in service to others.

10 HOUSE MOVE FROM HELL

February 2007

I lived in a beautiful five-bedroom house, which we sold to move to the country. Kevin, my husband, had become ill, and I told him I would happily live in a cardboard box. At that 3am hospital visit, Kevin was on a cardio machine monitoring his heart. No, it wasn't a heart attack; it was stress. Stress kills, and a change of pace was in order.

It was a troubling time, and we entered an economic recession. House prices were stupidly high, and bidding wars pushed prices higher. Kevin accepted a redundancy; nothing was holding us in Bangor Co Down. We would live on what I earned. I guess we both had ideas of having chickens and planting potatoes, living off the land.

We sold our house very quickly, with enough to have a relatively small mortgage. But where would we go?

I had been to Randalstown a few weeks prior and fallen in love with the bridge, a beautiful feature of the town, and I suggested we look there. After contacting estate agents, the flyers for houses were in a daily stream. One particular house we went to see. Neither of us were blown away by it. And yet, daily, the same house was posted through our letter box. It became a joke between Kevin and me as I produced the house flyer that neither of us liked. Of course, it was a sign.

To cut a long story short, it was that very house we bought. Yes, it too went into a closed bidding situation, which we won by £50.

A three-bed bungalow set in a large half-acre plot down a shared country lane. It was downsizing, but it was going to be OK.

We relocated in February 2007, on a cold, rainy day, contracts were only exchanged at the last minute. It was dark at 5pm when we got the keys to our new home.

We lit the fire in the living room, and all slept on the sofas, huddling to keep warm. The house was cold and had been empty for some time. The doors didn't close; it was damp. Kevin and I worked hard to get the bedrooms sorted for the next day, and with that done, Kevin took ill. He had the flu, and not the good kind.

Boxes were everywhere, and I was somewhat depressed about our circumstances. What had we done? We had relocated to the sticks and knew no one.

I needed to consult with the spirit world. When Kevin was well again, I told him he needed to speak directly with my guides. And not to take any of this, don't worry, everything will be OK, stuff they always say!

Kevin is well versed in my trance states and has spoken with my guides. It was on their assurance that this move would be a good thing for us. And yet, here we were in what felt like the bleak mid-winter of a never-ending wilderness.

The boys attended a small country school of fewer than 50 pupils; practically a private education was at the time the only plus.

A few weeks later and Kevin had recovered. I sat on a hard-backed wooden chair in the living room. Kevin was on the sofa, and I set my intentions to connect with my guides. It can be hit or miss. You see, I have no control as to which guide will come through or even if they are available to chat.

It became clear from the guides that I had much work to do. The resounding words from Spirit were never to worry about the financial aspect; we would always have enough. Work opportunities would be available soon.

It was not long before we were in that financially worrying state I was afraid of. I sat at the kitchen table, glaring at the bills, and wondering how I would pay them.

11. MEET THE NEIGHBOURS

March 2007

The blankets slowly started to move of their own volition. Was it that movement that woke me up or the deafening silence, you know, that vacuum feeling?

I froze. I didn't move a muscle. My eyes darted around the velvet black of my bedroom, straining to see who was there and stretching my ears to hear. There was no source of light from anywhere. My breathing was not right; it was so very tight. That's what woke me up. I reached for my blue inhaler from the bedside table and administered the puffs that would ease my chest. Fully concentrating on taking the medication, not wanting to notice that feeling. I did not return the inhaler to the bedside table; no, I tucked it under my pillow.

This is when I wish I had put lights on the bedside tables. It was unnerving, this country life we had chosen. It was taking some getting used to. Note to self: more light in the bedroom, please.

Maybe I imagined it all. I waited. Yes, there it was again—that gentle pulling down of the blankets. There was no mistaking the presence of a spirit in the room! I pinched my arm hard to see if I was dreaming. You see, this was not the first experience of this kind. In fact, this was fast becoming a thing. I don't like it when I don't understand why it is happening.

We had only been in the house for less than a month when this all started. Kevin said I just needed to get used to the place and its noises, but there is a difference between house noises and the feeling of spirits watching you in your bed or pulling the covers off.

Sure, I should be ok with this kind of thing. After all, I am a medium. I talk to strangers all the time. Yes, that's on my terms as to how and when. This? This is something altogether different. This is beyond my control, and that I don't like.

Daisy, my beautiful four-legged companion, chose to sleep by the embers of the fire. Smart dog. She must have figured out there was something eerie happening. Note to self again. Must take the heads up from this clever dog in the future. Yes, there it was; it was happening again—the pull, the freeze, the feeling.

With a backward kick, I connected with Kevin's thigh. He muttered something and then turned over.

Then there was such an odd sensation. I had been so far on high alert—wide awake, like ten espresso coffees awake. A delightfully seductive, strange, warm exhaustion flooded my body and mind, and amid this experience, I fell into a deep, dreamless sleep. Totally out of the ordinary, rather extraordinary. Who falls asleep in the middle of a haunting? Exactly? But I did, and a blissful sleep it was too.

I awoke to the sounds of the dawn chorus; the sky just lighting up could be seen through the gaps in the curtains. I sat up in bed and rubbed my forearm. I lifted my pillow, retrieved the blue inhaler, and popped it on the bedside table. Yip, a big nip bruise was starting to form on my arm. I had nipped so hard that you could see the tiny pinpoint dots caused by broken capillaries under the skin. WHAT did it mean? What was all this about? It wasn't a case of sleep paralysis; the forearm proved that point!

The golden sunlight lit up the tidy bungalow in a joyous way. Sure, it was a cold, bitter morning, but it was dry, and the sun was shining. I noted that my breathing (asthma, which had not been behaving as it should) was so much easier, and the wheeze that had been a feature with me had actually gone. Perhaps I had received some healing during the wee hours of the morning. Whatever had happened last night had been helpful because I felt great.

Only three days later, Daisy had opted for the fireside again; who could blame her? It had been blowing a hoolie for the last two days.

Lamps had been placed on the bedside tables, so I didn't mind that Daisy wasn't beside me as I slept. The trustee light bulb armed me; if needed, I would leave it on all night. The "spookie ookies," as I call them, don't like the light.

I slept well until Kevin started yelling, "Who is that?" I am a relatively light sleeper; it comes with motherhood. You always have your ears open should one of your little darlings need you!

I switched the bedside lamp on, and the room filled with light.

Kevin had been asleep and then suddenly awoke. He was lying in bed in the darkness when he felt something jump on his chest. He said I know what it was. It was a child. But there is nothing here; he said as he scanned the room. He said he half thought it was one of our boys jumping into our bed. But that was just not the case. He was a bit bewildered because he knew he was awake.

This was Kevin's experience. I had been out for the count until he shouted, and I fell back to sleep with ease.

In light of the strange occurrence, we were both experiencing, we held a seance, just the two of us. That was all that was required.

It came to light that, yes, spirit people and children were drawn to the new occupants on the lane.

They were curious and somewhat delighted to have us there.

We, of course, had met the neighbours when we moved in some months ago. But now we were formally meeting our spiritual neighbours.

No, the house is not haunted. These were visitations, they stated. They apologised for disturbing us; they didn't realise just how sensitive we were. The other occupants that had lived there before us didn't bat an eyelid when they visited them, they said.

The planchette whizzed around the spirit board, pointing to the letters of the alphabet, and spelling out the details of who and how they were connected. The planchette only paused as one spirit left and a new soul wished to be acknowledged.

Anne, a young teenager, told us she connected directly to the land; her father, John, also in spirit, had bought the farm at the top of the lane. We called it the old farm. The house stands empty, with a new house built for the present owner, Henry. She explained that Brendan, her baby brother, jumped on Kevin's chest.

They were, of course, quite chatty, and friendly and welcomed us with open arms. There brother had built the house we had bought and all the family lived on the lane. So they would visit often. We thanked them for the communication and felt easier knowing that these spiritual experiences were friendly and helpful!

I asked about the strange sleeping feeling and the presence in the room. It was clear that they had no part in that experience, nor did they comment on what they felt it might be.

That experience, for the moment, is still a mystery.

Journal update January 2022

Anne died at the young age of fourteen. Her brother was only a baby. This was verified later when checking out the history and validity of the communication.

It would be a whole three years before Anne would make herself known again. Three hefty knocks at the bedroom door at 3 am in

September 2010 signified the passing over of her youngest sister Sheena.

She visited in the same way at the same time, announcing the deaths of her siblings two to three days before the event. Anne informed us on December 31, 2019, that another sibling was to pass, and Henry Devlin, the eldest brother, died in January 2020.

12. A GYPSY CARAVAN

March 2007

My mobile rang in its melodious tone, and I picked it up. It was the old Nokia phone (I actually still have it in a drawer in my bedroom). Is that the fortune teller? I don't classify myself as that, but hey, it was an enquiry. Yes, I said, how can I help you? I made a booking, and I quickly arranged the utility room into an office. Nestled behind my psychic sofa was the tumble dryer and washing machine, carefully covered with lovely material. It was the best I could do. The fridge freezer stood tall in the corner. It is what it is.

The clients came in dribs and drabs at first, with every penny carefully put away for the bills. Within a number of weeks of hard graft, we had enough to pay the outstanding bills and take a trip to the movies.

The spirit guides had been right; not a lotto win, but opportunities to work.

Work increased exponentially as word got out about the Fortune Teller. I worked all over the country, driving to houses for groups with individual bookings at home in the small utility room.

It was clear to me that a separate space was required as bouncy, inquisitive children sometimes interrupted the private sessions.

A large static caravan was the practical answer, and it arrived swiftly, a most welcome gift from my mother.

The caravan I adored. It was private, but I was now also a cliche.

The large, static, two-bedroom caravan sat just outside the back door, secured by large chains to the concrete as high winds could easily lift it, and at times during storms, I often thought I would end up like Dorothy in the Wizard of Oz.

I redecorated the interior, pulled out all the fittings, and had a lovely room with two sofas and a Reiki bed for spiritual healing.

Many happy psychic years were spent in that caravan. Many tears shed, healings and, at times, small psychic workshops.

The spirit guides were right. I had a lot of work to do, and my training was ongoing. I was studying for my certificates at the time with the Spiritualist National Union, which took me away to England for weeks on end of training in various colleges and locations.

My role as a mother had changed. Kevin was now the Mummy Daddy and had to take on the role of both parents as I worked tirelessly to keep us all financially afloat.

House parties across the province filled my diary, and I would arrive home in the wee hours of the morning exhausted. It must have been lonely for Kevin, with me gone most of the day and many evenings. It was worrying, too, as I would be crossing flashpoint areas where The Troubles could be found. I could not have done it without him. He has always been my rock.

13. FRANCIS IS HERE

June 2007

One particular house party in North Belfast, an area known as a flash point. For the Troubles would stir in some places.

After all this time, anger still remains. Mutual distrust and suspicions still exist between the communities, and at times, this tension comes to a head like a grossly pussy angry pustule. On occasion this tension erupts and, in rare cases, heals. Where there is such hatred, the spot never mends as it is picked and picked to become inflamed and angry. I am not a political entity, but I see where healing is required and hope that the resentment will dissipate in time.

Needless to say, I crossed peace lines and entered places that some would not dare to go.

I was greet warmly. The house was immaculate, and I was led to a small bedroom just off the landing. I could see the staircase from where I sat on a single bed. I could see my car being watched by a small boy through the window. The other cars on the street sat proudly on concrete breeze blocks; their wheels had been secreted away.

One by one, I would see my clients in the privacy of the bedroom. Some seek guidance from their loved ones, and others need direction from which the cards and my psychic insights would give.

I was reading my last client from the group a kindly gentleman in his 40s. No sooner had I laid the cards out than I felt his mother's presence. I said your mum's here; she keeps saying Francis is here. Frances is here.

The gentleman quickly started to collect my cards, laid out on the bed, and popped them into the suede Indian pouch bag I keep them in. I was stunned a little, and my eyes gazed through the gap in the bedroom door to the stairs. Everything was in slow motion.

A lit lamp still attached to its electrical supply seemed to float in mid-air and suddenly crashed to the floor.

"Quick," the man said. "Francis is my brother; he is back from the pub and drunk."

I could hear muffled shouts, pleading, and angry words. I really don't recall how I ended up crouched behind the large black wheelie bin in the yard with the gentleman I was attempting to read. But it would seem that Francis had a great aversion to psychic mediums that day, and his drunken threats of shooting, etc., were somewhat unsettling.

I was stunned, disoriented, and confused.

I found my way to the back gate, stood in front of my car, and attempted to pay the lad a couple of pounds, for which he refused. He, too, could hear the commotion and was in no hurry to go home. I drove back to Randalstown and tried to process the evening.

Flashbacks to the angry scene flooded my mind as I could, from my hidden position, see into the kitchen window. Had I not been so quickly removed; I would not have been able to tell this story.

I got home, sat with my coffee, and spoke with the spirit world. I was a little shaken and scared if I am totally honest.

I was told *that not a hair on my head would ever be harmed. I was to be secure in the knowledge that I would always be protected.*

In hindsight, it was true I had been altered to danger, and I had been kept safe, a little ruffled, but I came to no physical harm.

This of course was a rare event for I was well received by all communities.

14. MANIFESTING A THICKER SKIN

Demonstrating in spiritual churches and teaching in Scotland and England filled my diary. I was living out of a suitcase and sleeping in lodgings or kindly parishioners' homes. It was far from a glamorous life. The pay wasn't great, but it was better than nothing, and it fulfilled a requirement for the certificates as a set number of church services needed to be assessed by the Spiritualist National Union.

My first public demonstration (not church-related) was held near my home in Antrim. It was a real eye-opener, as with a church demonstration, those who attend are already versed in the ins and outs of Spiritual Connections, not so in a demonstration for the general public. Oh no, that was a whole different ballgame.

During one of my straight-line trance sessions with Kevin, my Spiritual Team urged me to organise a demonstration. I must say it was nerve-wracking. Advertising in local papers, I had no idea that the event would be so successful. My flower sentience had developed further, and it was the first time I was to share my gift in such a public arena with no ties to the Spiritual Churches I had been serving over the years.

We got a babysitter for the boys, and Kevin came and supported me, taking the money at the door, a whopping £10 pp. The room hire alone was £250, and I calculated that if we had 50 people, it would be a success. Instead, we had 100.

I was sick to my stomach standing in front of an audience that large. In the churches I had served, you would be lucky to get an audience of thirty, so this was a huge leap.

I started nervously explaining what I do and need not have been nervous at all. The spiritual energy lifted and transported me, and before I knew it, the event was over, and happy people were exclaiming how great it was that I had shared my gift.

My Facebook page had recently been created, and I happily posted pictures of my event.

I was ill-prepared for the social media fallout: angry comments, abuse, and threats from invisible people who did not dare to sign their names. Trolls are what we call them now. They didn't have a name when I started my internet journey. Sadly, that is what is now the norm for me.

There, nestled in a Facebook messenger window behind blank profile pictures, were a plethora of horrible, nasty statements. I was a devil worshipper. I was praying for the weak and vulnerable. I should be ashamed of myself. Those are tame, for there were uglier, vile, and vulgar messages too.

They knocked me sideways; as a sensitive being, I cried for two solid days, proclaiming that a job at a checkout or stacking shelves would suit me better.

I sent my thoughts to the Spirit World for help as I hid under my duvet. My computer and phone were switched off. Get up and get on with it. They said that I should take no longer than three days. Wipe my tears and know that I am loved.

I tentatively turned on my computer and switched on my phone after three days as instructed.

Yes, there were a few more nasty messages that I quickly deleted, as I did not dare to read them. But then, yes, then, there were the messages of gratitude. Some were attending that event and wished to book private sittings—some more lovely messages of how that special communication had changed their outlook and fear of death. One lady said, "I never got to say goodbye to my husband; you gave me an opportunity for closure." She thanked me for the red rose she received. She said you were right; he only bought her red roses, and this one was special and would be pressed and put into a frame next to his picture.

The Spirit World basically told me to put my big girl panties on and get on with it. With their help, I am still trying to manifest that thicker skin.

15. HEAVENLY VISITS

January 2019

I was having a bit of a restless sleep last night, anxious and worried. Perhaps I was running away from an unseen monster in my dream or was it that I was back in school and I had forgotten my homework, or worse, my underwear. I cannot, for the life of me, remember what had me tossing and turning, but I suddenly became aware of stillness to the torment of the emotional waves I had been surfing, and I settled into a calm and safe space.

Daisy, my dog had rested her head on my hand. Her cold, wet nose nudged at my hand and I absently stroked her silky-smooth fur and murmured, "I'm OK Daisy love, I'm OK." She gently nudged with her nose again and gave a muffled soft whoof. With half opened eyes, I saw the crest of white on her chest and the sparkle of her wise eyes as she tilted her head and retreated back from the bed to find her spot on the floor by my bed, and I drifted off into a deep and easy sleep.

This morning I awoke and looked at the brass bed knob that held Daisy's collar. Her ashes in an amber Victorian sweet jar on my bedside table had sat there for eight years. Fat, hot, silent tears spilled down my cheeks and dropped from my chin to my chest. The pain never ceases to amaze me that I can feel this way after all this time.

Lu Lu, the not so miniature Schnauzer, bounced into the room, her tongue sticking out at the side of her mouth in a soppy silly way as she eyed up my husband's sock, and before I could reach my feet to the floor, the sock had been taken and a game of chase was in play.

I wiped the tears from my face as I followed a very playful fur baby to the back door with a large thick woollen sock clenched tightly in her mouth. I had no chance of retrieving that now. I opened the door and off she went, followed by Bella, a Belgian Malinois, who came from nowhere, nearly knocking me off my feet.

I made myself a coffee and, as I sipped the hot steaming liquid, my thoughts went back to Daisy and her visit. I recalled in detail how soft her fur was, the way she nudged my hand, how in life she was never far from my side. She was a true and loyal friend. I am so grateful that she came to visit.

What was the visit about? I guess it is about true and loyal friends. I love easily, I forgive quickly, and yes, I suffer fools. I don't want to change myself, but I do need to protect my gentle heart from those who would wish to manipulate, use, or harm me. Daisy was giving me a warning, as all great friends do, and it wasn't too long after I found out the who and why. We in life will meet many people who will betray us. The pain and the experience of this hurt an essential marker as to how deep we love and trust. And essentially the time taken to recover from such wounds.

I often find that dogs in spirit attend my demonstrations. It is a way of letting me know that the person I am speaking with is vulnerable. Arguably, it could be considered that all those attending my events are vulnerable. When a spirit dog appears by them, it lets me know that they have been subjected to or about to be exposed to a betrayal.

I remember one night in Enniskillen at the Killyhevlin Hotel. A spirit puppy walked down the aisle and sat at the feet of a lady I was speaking with. Her husband was in spirit, and I was delivering a heartfelt message to her. I mentioned the dog and she gasped. I said the dog had been helped over to the spirit world, though I didn't find an illness. She replied that she backed the car over it several times by mistake. It was no laughing matter, yet laughter erupted as she explained in comic detail the horror of the story.

The same lady then went on to book a reading with me several days after the demonstration in Enniskillen. I told her the puppy in spirit came to warn her about a disturbing event and that someone she cared for was about to betray her. She confirmed that her then boyfriend had been caught cheating on her the day after the event. She was without a doubt upset. Her reading explored other opportunities were harmony and balance in relationships would be found.

But, dogs, indeed, are unquestionably loyal. A visit from my Daisy is always welcome even if at times these visits hold a darker message.

I cast my mind back to my visit and wonder just how strange it is that when Daisy visits, I am never sad at the time. It is as if she had never left at all.

16. LIFFORD OLD COURTHOUSE

15th June 2019

It was that strange silence that awoke me. I don't know if you have ever experienced it. Yes, it is hard to describe because it feels like a vacuum; there is no sound; and yet there is a notable sense of pressure; a spiritual tension, like holding your breath.

She stood at the bottom of my big brass bed, flanked by two smaller shadows I assumed were children. I could not see the faces clearly, but then again, I never do. The icy chill followed, and I was fully engaged and present.

Time seemed to stop as I glanced sideways at the green flashing 3:33am. from the Alexa device on the bedside table. The small illumination adds no further definition nor detail to the uninvited guests.

As alarming as it would seem, I have become accustomed to these visits, especially when attending a supernatural activity or paranormal investigation with a group of people. It would seem those spirit people from whatever location I am attending have paid me a visit. There is little to no communication during their initial contact other than that they are there.

This ghostly etiquette has become rather a familiar occurrence over the years. I personally believe it is their way of checking me out, for they know I am coming.

I hosted a supernatural activity on the 15th of June 2019 at the old Lifford Courthouse. It is a rather strange space; not entirely all bad, but some elements of the history of the building and its goings on are rather nasty.

Lifford Old Courthouse was built in 1746 and is situated in the capital of Donegal, which, once upon a time, hosted some of the most hardened criminals in the country.

Steeped in history, his venue is now a museum. Creepy wax figures placed in reputably haunted areas have been said to move and add a ghoulish and sinister feeling to the building.

Of course, hangings were a regular occurrence, and the souls of those who perished often did nothing more than steal food.

The cells at the Old Courthouse were particularly active. The apparition who had come to see me in my own home then revealed who she was. Her name, whilst living, had been Mary. She had never been a criminal. She was deemed unfit and a lunatic, although she was far from that in reality. She spent her life incarcerated within these walls until death took her, along with what was left of her sanity. In all accounts, she was very helpful during the paranormal investigation and most obliging when asked to make this or that move. She was rather a lovely lady who had a terrible existence.

The children were from the debtor's prison and, sadly, didn't make the cut for deportation. Their illness and fever were too great, and they perished where they lay.

The most haunted event was successful, and all those attending had their fill of spooky goings on. As always, at these places, I sit quietly after the event and offer my gratitude for their help and the work they do as spirits.

30th June 2022

Three years had passed, and I once again stood on the steps of the Old Courthouse in Lifford. My first thoughts were about Mary and her sad story. I wondered if she knew I was coming.

The event room was just perfect on the first floor, and the chairs were carefully spaced, still allowing for social distancing. The beautiful tall sash windows had been freshly painted shut. Attendees filtered in and quietly took their seats, a well-mannered group eager to enjoy the demonstration of mediumship.

The event started promptly at 8pm, and after the first few spiritual messages had been delivered, the lights in the room started to flicker off and on rather dramatically. Loud banging noises could be heard from the cells.

Some in the room started to get fearful, asking what was happening. I knew it was just the ghostly inhabitants recognising my energy. I told the audience not to worry that the building remembered me and that this was how they were welcoming me back as an old friend.

For I had felt the friendship and warmth of a woman, whom I had met so briefly in spirit form again. Throughout the demonstration that night, the lights did flicker and groans, knocks, and whistles could be heard by all who attended. All in all, a rather fabulous night with spirit.

There is so much more to our world than what it appears to be.

Our loved ones who have crossed over into Heaven have huge amounts of access to our world. They cannot only communicate across dimensions but can also make their presence known to us in ways that use all our senses.

I know the smell of my father's cologne. The hint of cinnamon is my maternal grandmother's. The smell of Matey Bubble bath is my fraternal grandmother's. Mothballs are my Aunty Olive. The list for me is endless, as I am sure it is for you.

Our loved ones find countless ways to tell us how much we are loved, guided, and supported from above.

You are truly never alone.

17. I AM READY TO GO

February 2016

It was 3:40 AM as I battled with my nebuliser, a device I had become dependent on as my asthma grew increasingly difficult. With hands both shaking and weak, I tore open the capsule holding the solution that would open my airways and let me breathe. Once the contents were safely secured in the device, I strapped the mask onto my face and waited. This was the second time I had been nebulising in half an hour, and yes, I was deeply concerned. I looked across the bed at my husband, who was blissfully sleeping. His chest rose and fell to a beautiful rhythm of contentment and ease. I really didn't want to have to wake him; he had sat up with me the last two nights, and he was exhausted. He slept soundly. The hiss and splutters of the machine didn't stir him. As I sat in the darkness of the bedroom awaiting the moment the medication would give me relief, a strange yet familiar sense was stirring. Yes, it was the Spirit world perceived in a different way. At first I thought, OK, it's my time. I'm tired, weary, and done in. Take me, I'm ready. I had no fear whatsoever. I was ready to leave. I knew I would meet my beautiful children and loving husband again. I was ready for the off, prepared to let go and let God.

A sensation and feeling coupled with a knowing encompassed me completely and the image of a lady I knew to be Vi Kipling, a tutor of mine many years ago, flooded my mind. What's going on here? In all honesty, I was expecting my father to escort me to the world beyond.

I recalled my first meeting with this lady at Arthur Findlay College well over a decade ago. She was a giant of a character held in a tiny, frail frame. She had an unwavering trust in and knowledge of the Spirit. Her voice was strong even though her words were punctuated at times with an uneasy breathlessness as she introduced herself to the class (I believe it was one of the many teacher training sessions I had attended). She reminded us of our duty to self and to spirit. We were the tutors of the future. I remember at that time feeling ill prepared and full of self-doubt. Was I worthy? Did I know enough? Was this really my path?

And now in my bedroom, years after her passing, she was flooding my mind with her brilliance with the oddest, most curious sensation, like being both hot and cold at the same time, but ultimately comforting, sweeping through my whole being. My shoulders and back, so hunched and raised, began to loosen, and relax. I felt an ease in my chest and an openness in my lungs that let the air flow effortlessly. I could breathe. All the while, the image of Vi Kipling was steadfast and true within my mind.

"Come on girl, you've got work to do," was the message, and a stream of images passed through my mind of the countless ways we today communicate and exchange information... "This is the way forward," she said, and I, of course, just said, "OK, I'm ready teach me."

From what I recall, way back then, on the course I was taking, I was indeed ill prepared. I had originally booked on to a psychic art class with a dear friend. How I got changed so quickly was the work of another tutor who recognised something within me and very quickly had the paperwork sorted. I must add that course changing is rather messy business, and costly too. Within a blink of an eye, a nod of the head, paperwork had been exchanged, former course organisers informed, and there I was on a new course with no additional cost to me.

I was now on the Tutoring Training Course with Vi Kipling to be my tutor. I recall a large crowd of eager students waiting to present their lesson plans and profiles, armed with laptops, printers, and handouts from previous courses. I, on the other hand, had some colouring pencils, chalks, and some stunning watercolour paint with a beautiful arrangement of paintbrushes.

I met some lovely spiritual people that week. Some were indeed rather gifted, others not so, but kindness is by far my favourite trait in a human being. We were split into two groups of twenty or more and herded into our rooms. Vi delivered a talk in a breathless, yet clear and precise way. I think she had COPD or asthma. I didn't dare to ask. To be honest, I was a little frightened of her, and for the first time in my life, I felt my palms sweat.

What had I done? I could be colouring in relaxing with my friend in a Psychic Art Class, and here I was listening to this amazing woman who had been born into spiritualism, sat in circles with greatly talented spiritualist mediums that I had only read about. Vi had written many books on a vast number of topics I had great interest in. And here she was explaining what we were to be tasked with. To say I was in awe of this lady would be an understatement. All in all, we were to present to her and the class from a title that would be given to us later that day for a workshop or seminar, from the poster we designed, the advert that we would present, the location we would choose, the cost it would incur, and most importantly, the course lesson plan and supportive documents, aka the handouts.

After a few gasps from some of the students, I felt a little better. There is one thing about me I know, and that is I am resourceful. I'm not bad at PowerPoint, nor would I struggle with design. I noticed there was a flip chart in the corner of the room nearly glowing for attention, but I ignored it. The girls on reception were extremely lovely. They would most probably let me use their computer. In fact, they did, and I was sorted.

The titles that were handed out were rather straightforward. Over lunch, I got to meet the other students on my course. They had come from all over the world, China, the United States, and the length and breadth of England were represented, but I believe I was the only Northern Irish student on that course. Some students were chatty, friendly, and eager to share their ideas; others were poo-faced, secretive, and sadly up their own bottoms.

I won't bore you with the trials and tribulations of the additional tasks that were asked of us, but I was still preparing the presentation on the very flip chart I spotted earlier on the course at 3am.

The bulbs on the projector broke down at the last minute, sending students into an array of panic, disbelief, and, like me, a hundred other emotions. I was given my time slot to present in the morning, and I just knew the projector wouldn't be fixed by then. My PowerPoint presentation was useless.

My paints, colouring pencils, and chalks were just what was required to bring a flip chart to life. I presented my program with the flip chart the very next morning, tired but happy that I had completed the task with the materials I had brought... It would seem that the spirit world knew that paints and chalk and pencils were all that was required that week.

At the end of the course, the two groups met in the library where both tutors discussed and deliberated who the most outstanding student was from their group. A gentleman, actually a lovely fellow, was chosen from the other group. Vi Kipling started to talk, and the crowd, after all the clapping and cheering, fell silent. She started to talk about this outstanding student who was, by all accounts, just amazing. She talked about their fellowship with their other students, that they were pioneers breaking new ground, that they were the way forward with their dedication to spirit. There was more, of course, but I must admit I zoned out for a bit. I was so tired and I closed my eyes for just a moment. After all, I didn't know who she was speaking about.

To my surprise, she called my name. I was the one she thought was the way forward, and here she was in my bedroom telling me from the world of spirit that I had work to do. Obviously, it's not my time to go to the Spirit World.

I slept for a couple of hours, and when it was an appropriate hour, I phoned my friend, spiritual sister, and wise owl, Denise Butterworth.

18. WISE OWL

May 2016

Denise and I first met many years ago at Coberhill in Scarborough, England, although Denise would say we met first at Arthur Findlay College some years prior. However, where it was matters little now, the fact remains that we were destined to be firm friends who shared over 15 years of friendship. Denise lived in Todmorden, and I was in Bangor, Northern Ireland, at the time; we were both incredibly interested and thirsty for knowledge in all things trance and all things spirit. Denise, like myself, had a keen and inquiring mind. We believed that there had to be the presence and evidence of spirit intelligence at work.

We took every opportunity to take classes and seminars together. And if one could go to one course and the other couldn't, we shared between us what we learnt. We were both notorious gigglers, which at times got us into a little trouble, as the spirit world is rather serious business indeed. However, joy can be found in the smallest, most intense corners of serious work. I do believe that we learn more with laughter than with a firm and stern de-meaner. So, working alongside a kindred spirit, esteemed colleague with a joyful disposition was indeed a dream.

So let me tell you a little about Denise Butterworth. She was a brilliant trance medium with excellent perception mediumship and had, for as long as I knew her, wished to give her life to spirit work. She worked tirelessly for spirit in her spare time, working in churches across England, Scotland, and Northern Ireland, to name a few, for little or no money at all. Her dream was to give up her work as a full-time nurse practitioner (within a very busy practice in Bradford) and dedicate her life to working independently from the spiritualist churches as a full-time medium.

I supported her in every way I could, giving her handy hints on how to procure the right space to hold her trance workshop and how to advertise on social media. Denise had, of course, worked with many other mediums on residentials and was very popular in the UK, working side by side with those deemed to be the creme de la creme within the movement. Yet this did not affect her lack of confidence, which I have to say totally amazed me, despite my many attempts to get her to recognise her uniqueness and my awe at her very special brand of mediumship.

Many a time, Denise worked with me in Northern Ireland and on the supernatural activities of my most haunted evenings, which were always well attended and fun-filled with delight at how the intelligence of spirit would manifest. Physical mediumship had always been a passion for us both and, in a way, made us closer than sisters. Not only did we study together, attending many classes together in college, where we both received our last award, the CSNUt, which was a two-year teaching programme. We worked together as often as we could on workshops and residentials organised by myself. Denise was always a hit with the developing Irish mediums, so patient, nurturing, and honest. It is true that working with her never seemed a chore, for it was such a treat and a joy to be in each other's presence.

After my visitation with Vi Kipling, I phoned Denise immediately to share with her the experience and ponder on the meaning of the visit and how it was that I should move forward electronically. Yes, I can find my way around a computer, but I am certainly no wiz. We deliberated on how mediumship for the 21st Century would move forward through

ITC (Instrumental Trance Communication). We had heard that great things were happening in Germany, and try as we may, we could not find the same thing happening in Ireland or the UK.

When Denise finally made the plunge to organise her first workshop, she was nervous and excited, not about the teaching but about the financial commitment and the advertising she would have to do. She had to do something she had never done before, which in some ways involved her blowing her own trumpet. Within moments of her tentative post on Facebook, her course was full with deposits paid by expectant and excited developing mediums eager to learn at the knee of a master. I call her Master, and I know she will be cringing in the world of spirit right now, but I was privileged to know the wealth of experience, knowledge, and understanding of spirit she had.

Her first workshop had been organised in May, and indeed, she was so very looking forward to meeting her students. She never did deliver that course; she died a couple of days beforehand, leaving a huge void in the Yorkshire district of the Spiritualist National Union. She passed away in the early hours of Sunday morning. I knew she had been unwell, but I never could have imagined a life without her in it. I had spoken with her on the Saturday night previous. I was running a trance workshop that Sunday, and all my students remarked on the very special presence in the room. I didn't investigate that presence thoroughly; I just assumed it was a new guide to my spirit team. I was in the flow of teaching and didn't wish to investigate the presence that was so very evident. It was later that I found out that Denise had been placed on a life support machine. But I knew within my heart that she had already departed this earth early Sunday morning and she had been the unseen visitor in my class.

My personal loss and grief at losing such a dear friend and spiritual sister was profound and deepened by my own gift, for at every turn I heard her voice, in the still of my own soul, she came to me reassuringly. Losing a spiritual sister was devastating but my gruelling work schedule left me little or no time to grieve. As a healer, I knew the stages of grief. The denial, anger, bargaining, depression, and acceptance after all those that seek my special talent are also grieving. Here it was that my deep-felt empathy for all my clients was very much in focus. There was something to be gained by my loss. As I worked deeper into the feeling of greater love, knowledge, and acceptance, I noticed a shift in my mind.

My visitation with Vi Kipling and the images that I was shown were more about communication with spirit than physical mediumship and how we today communicate with each other. The emphasis was on how to work remotely using this technology. At the time, I must admit, Denise and I were perplexed. Looking back now, Vi Kipling was giving me a nudge to ready myself.

Vi had been very involved with internet chat rooms at the dawn of the internet superhighways. I had shied away from things I knew little about, so I had to learn about all the above, to incorporate them in some way, for apparently this was how I would move forward with my work for spirit.

Of course, I had demonstrated online with the SNUI. How could I have forgotten this? In fact, my first ever online demonstration was with Vi Kipling herself. I remember being so nervous sitting in my office with my laptop in Randalstown Co Antrim. Vi was the inspirational speaker and I was the demonstrating medium. The chairperson was welcoming all those to the virtual service, and Vi had private messaged me, and I had told her I was extremely nervous as it was my first time on the internet and I might press the wrong button whilst demonstrating. She eased my anxiety with her wicked sense of humour. The service was a success; there were no interruptions on the internet, and no rogue buttons were accidentally pushed. Since then, I have been an online tutor for the SNUI.

In the wake of COVID-19, everything went online. Private sittings were conducted via Skype, Zoom, Facebook Messenger, and FaceTime. Demonstrations were all on-line via Zoom video conferencing. It would seem that Vi Kipling was giving me the heads up as to the way forward.

Denise has often visited me and her friendship and encouragement often felt when I need it most.

19. FORGET ME NOT

2021

Not all the flowers at my demonstration are claimed during the event. No, some are too sensitive, too embarrassing, or just plain too sad. I do not get upset or concerned; there are always valid reasons that come to light later.

I stood before my audience (the venue and date are of little relevance). As usual, I opened up my demonstration with an explanation of how the night would flow.

I explained the table before me. Adorned with beautiful flowers, dressed in ribbons and trinkets pertinent to the spirit communicator(s) and the recipient. I discuss how each flower may be linked to one or more individuals from the spirit world; it is up to the audience to claim their loved ones from the evidence that is given. Yes, I do sometimes go directly to individuals in the audience. I don't necessarily like to do so, as some people do not wish to participate, merely attend.

One night in Londonderry, I learnt this the hard way, some eight years ago, when a daughter wished to speak to her mother. The mother did not want to participate. The message was a beautiful one of love and happiness. The recipient, so entrenched in her grief, was less appreciative of the direct approach and made it known. It was embarrassing, as she lashed out during the demonstration, claiming I was being a bully—something I am not. The upset lady contacted me later via text, letting me know that she was horrified that I had brought her daughter through so publicly. She had booked me for a private one-on-one and was now canceling it because she felt I had bullied her. Needless to say, I was distraught. I reflected carefully on the evening, and in no way or form would I have said my behaviour was anything other than loving and caring. For that very reason, I very rarely go directly to the recipients in the audience. Arguably, one would defend my actions and say she attended an event of spirit communication; what was she expecting? Nonetheless, it is what it is. At times, people in pain can be difficult to understand, and it is essential to be kind at all costs.

The event I am talking about now was well attended, albeit socially distanced. Some attendees wore masks; others didn't, as restrictions for COVID-19 were being relaxed.

Mental health is a thing. Regardless of the era we are living in, trauma exists throughout.

It was the last flower on the table; all the others had been received gleefully, gratefully, with joy and sadness as they were reconnected to their loved ones.

It was the time for the little blue forget-me-not flower. She had been so patient, sitting at my table and in my mind. She is most memorable for her story, which struck a chord in my heart.

I don't always remember my demonstrations or what was said during them. I am in an altered state of awareness with one foot in heaven and the other on earth as I pass the spirit messages on. But this little flower had a huge impact on me.

My flower sentience has altered with time, so I hold the essence of the spirit people within my mind whilst picking the flowers. Only once the flowers are fully dressed and ready for the demonstration do they allow me to see more. During the demonstration, I will touch the flower.

Once I have tapped into the flower's energy, the full depth and flavour of the soul steps forward.

I touched the last solitary flower on the table, a tiny blue flower tied with a pink ribbon, and the communicator stepped forward.

She was a petite-framed lady who informed me that she had suffered with dementia. She told me of her family; she had two children she loved with all her heart. She talked of her grandchildren with great pride, stating one was a teacher and others were in the caring profession. She said she was with her husband in spirit and was delighted to be reunited with the love of her life. She talked of the loneliness she had experienced since he had parted some 30 years or so before. He had died of cancer.

No one was taking the tiny blue flower. Not one hand went up. I continued.

She talked again about how lonely she had felt in the home. She had been taken to a care home. You see, her house was sold, and she could never return to it again. She briefly mentioned visits from her grandchildren and her son when she first went in, which seems to have ended there—no more visits.

Still, no hands claiming this lady. I then felt that her story would indeed be more powerful than I could ever have imagined.

Urged on by my gentle spirit communicator, I carried on with her captivating story. Her love of pastel colours, the art of being a keen seamstress in her day, how she was saddened by the falling out of her children. The issues with the family home being sold and unfairness in the financial split had caused a deeper wound and a larger rift.

Not a living soul in the room stirred, hanging on every word. There was a shift of spiritual energy, and in my mind, she was joined by others who in life had had the same life experience as her. It was as if she was being supported spiritually by them—urged to tell her story.

I knew, at this stage, there would be no one claiming her as their own.

Even so, I carried on.

She talked about her room and the window where she sat in the care home. A large tree was outside her window, and she could see the changing of the seasons as the leaves turned brown and fell from the branches. She was visually impaired by cataracts but could still see shapes and colours. Covid was in the home, and her meals were brought in and taken away. There were no visits, no company, and everyone in the care home was in their own rooms.

I could see how the audience was reacting to this communication, as some wiped tears from their eyes.

The lady ended her communication by saying that from time to time, her deceased husband visited, and she was glad to join him. She told me she had not died alone; a lovely care assistant was with her, holding her hand. She slipped away gracefully and was delighted that her time on earth was at an end. She was not lonely now and was truly happy.

No one claimed the lady. I took the forget-me-not home at the end of the evening. I placed the flower in a small crystal egg cup, sent a special thought to the lady, and thanked her for her bravery and communication.

Two days later, I received a phone call. The person had attended the event mentioned above. The granddaughter said there had been bad feelings in the family, and a huge row had split them. They could not visit their grandmother due to the pandemic restrictions at that time, and FaceTime or video calls could not be made; Granny did not have such a device. There was an acceptance that she would be cared for whilst she was in the home, and everyone went on with their lives.

The granddaughter was clearly upset, and she felt guilty that she did not visit or try to communicate with the care home at the time. In fact, she stated, regretfully, that she had forgotten all about her until that night of the demonstration. She went on to explain that at the demonstration, she didn't even know if her granny was dead or not, which is why she never raised her hand to claim her.

It was only when she spoke to other family members that she found out about her grandmother's death and burial some months ago. She was devastated that she had missed her grandmother's final goodbye.

She asked if her granny was angry with her, and I assured her that it surely wasn't the case and that her communication that night at the demonstration was only of love and to let everyone know she was happy.

As the phone call ended, she asked me what the flower her granny had picked was. I said it was a forget-me-not. The flower itself is a message to her granddaughter to always remember her with love.

As I write this in my journal, I am saddened that many older individuals during this horrid pandemic may have felt so lonely. Some passed to spirit without family surrounding them as each health and care facility practiced different policies.

May we never forget the love we have for our family and the love they have for us.

20. SYNCHRONICITY OF SPIRIT

Cookstown, 16th February 2017

I was halfway through the demonstration. I was on a raised stage with the audience, some sitting theatre style, whilst others sat at tables dotted around the room. The young waitress with a tray filled with piping hot coffees and teas was weaving around the crowd to get to her customers. I watched her as I shared the link I had to spirit.

A lovely lady from spirit wanted to connect with her carer. She talked about her carer with great affection. She said her carer was a daily treat and how fond she had grown of her during their time together. She described her home and her illnesses and how she enjoyed the young girl who was so patient with her. She had a large family and many grandchildren, with no time for an old lady in a wheelchair. She had suffered a stroke, and her speech had been affected. She told me the carer's name, which I called out: Ciara.

I watched the waitress as she stopped in her tracks. Regain her posture and deliver her tray to the customers. The waitress then very slowly walked back from her customer's table. Her head was bent down, trying to be invisible.

As she crossed the front of the stage, I said, "Excuse me, but are you Ciara? She nodded emotionally. I said you haven't always been a waitress, have you? She nodded again. "Did you look after a lady called Evelyn?" I asked. She said yes, choking back a sob. Tears streamed down her face.

I said she just wanted to say thank you for all the lovely time you both spent; she thought the world of you.

The waitress welled up with tears, said thank you, and quickly walked away. At the end of the evening, Ciara approached me.

She thanked me for the message and confirmed that she had been a carer for Evelyn for a year. When she passed, she found it too hard to return to her role as a carer and had taken a job as a waitress. She was delighted to be remembered and had more than a thousand questions about the afterlife, for she had never really thought about what happens after death.

I marvel at the synchronicity of spirit. For it just does not end there. During private sessions I see patterns in the work for weeks on end I will receive all manners of the same version of events.

For instance, I had a number of readings reflecting the same theme. Family feuds.

Toxicity in all its forms can happen in any relationship type. Work Colleagues, Ex-Lovers, So Called Friends, Neighbours and the list goes on. What I believe is the hardest expression is that which is experienced in families.

Unlike any other group, family members are special, because we are related to them in someway, and that may be much harder to deal with because we think we can't get away from them. For there will be many occasions when all the family come together, weddings, funerals, anniversary, the holidays.

These spiritual lessons are never one-sided I am always reminded of that we are all human and flawed and no soul is without help nor love.

It remind me of Disney's Lilo and Stitch Ohana - No one gets left behind or forgotten.

21. CLIENTS IN PAIN

September 2017

I had a client visit me. They were indeed in a world full of emotions, anger and hurt from the very recent breakdown of a twenty-something marriage. They agreed with all I had to say and stated it was a true account of their situation (bear in mind please that this client had driven some distance of over an hour to come to my office). I could see the pain and anger in their auras, which were pulsing a dark, muddy red. This is what I usually see when I'm working with people who are in extreme pain.

I knew that my words of hope as I reached into the future of my client would not be heard as their anger was too strong, fuelling other more negative emotions and harbouring rather nasty thoughts of revenge for their now ex-partner.

They left just as angry and hostile, ignoring my words and my time as they stormed out of my office, ranting that they had given them everything.

In situations like this, there is nothing one can do more than lend a sympathetic ear, hoping that the rant will be exhausted and healing can begin. This was not the case, as their anger spilled over me with a verbal barrage of abuse, accusations, and demands that made little or no sense.

As the door slammed behind them, I prayed that they would have a safe journey home and that their pain would subside to awaken a new happiness.

I was not fazed by the outburst, nor was I upset. Had they not traveled so far, I would have declined the reading, stating that they were not quite ready for a sitting and giving them another date and time.

I recall a similar reading when a lady came to visit me in my Ballyholme office some 15 years back. She was a lovely lady but her circumstances were to change dramatically. When I informed her that her life was to undergo such extreme changes and urged her to ensure all paperwork and signatures were in place, she screamed and shouted at me. I was left shaking at the abuse.

Six months later, she contacted me for another reading. On arrival, she apologised profusely for her behaviour. I had been right, and she was ready to listen. This time it was for mediumship and her lovely partner, who had died six months earlier, came through. He had died from a brain tumour, and they were in the middle of moving house. The paperwork had not been completed and any insurance policies were no longer valid. The mortgage fell through and she was left to find a new home, this time alone. He insisted from the spirit world that her life was not over but just beginning. She came to me again in my Randalstown office. Her lovely partner from spirit congratulated her on her new relationship and happiness, as he had in some way been the matchmaker and was indeed delighted with her union.

When I am mentoring students, I remind them that such clients exist, that pain and grief can cause all manner of behaviours, and not to react to anger but to keep calm at all costs. I also remind them that safety of self is paramount.

One rather awful experience was with a man. He had to come to my office for a psychic reading. He wanted to know if he would immigrate to Australia. When reading for him, I revealed that he would soon be unemployed, that the industry was making radical changes and that he, amongst others, would be let go.

I told him that his actions after the event would be the cause of a failed visa. He became angry and threatening, and I was glad he left, even though he didn't pay me.

His anger frightened me to the extent that I now have a security system in place. He returned 11 months later. I recognised his aura. Yes, I read for him. My husband was close by. Should I feel fearful? Yes, he had been made redundant from his job. A court case now ensued for a drink driving offence, which was going to leave him without a licence and any hope for a visa. This time he paid me and left without abuse.

But there are times when I simply just can't connect. As frustrating as it is for me, it is also upsetting and worrying for the client. I don't believe any of the clients I have genuinely been unable to read for have had untimely deaths, run over by buses , etc. For whatever reason, I just have not been able to connect to their energy. I usually know within seconds if I am able to read for someone. It doesn't happen too often, but it does happen.

I had just finished off a rather fabulous reading and was about to take my last client, their sister, who was waiting in the car, when a huge wave of nausea hit me so badly I had to retreat to the bathroom.

I explained to my client how I was feeling and that there was no way I could continue to work. I asked if she could let her sister know I was ill and that I would arrange another time for her.

From the bathroom in my office I could hear the shouts of abuse from a woman who was clearly more than angry. I left the bathroom to come face to face with a woman who just needed to let me know just how upset they were and what they thought of me. With a flurry of arms waving and words I wouldn't utter nor type, she left the office with the door swinging on its hinges. I could hear the car wheels spinning on the stones outside with a roar and she had left.

I shut the door quietly and realised I no longer felt sick. Had I just been saved? Most likely the case.

Now I have to admit that the very same extreme sensations of nausea has been experienced before. I actually went to my doctor to get check out and nothing could be found wrong with me.

I now recognise it to be a warning. As unpleasant as it is at the time, there is no ignoring it. When I cancel the reading(s) the symptoms miraculously disappear.

22. TRANCE HEALING

September 2012

I was very excited to be invited to a private trance course run by a prestigious English Medium. It was held in a private home in England. The course itself was not advertised it was by special request only. Those attending were working mediums in their own right some whose talents were rather extraordinary. It really was a rather interesting bunch of accomplished women. Among those chosen to attend was my Wise Owl Denise.

This was not the first time I had been selected to attend such a courses, no, I had been lucky enough to be invited to many of its kind over the years of my development. The majority of the attendees held awards for their mediumship with the Spiritual National Union, and like me had travelled far to attend. Here it was that those attending knew what would be asked of them and they were willing to stretch, share and learn with the support of group.

Trance has always been a favourite of mine the healing side sadly too passive for my liking. It is Physical Trance that excites me the most.

Denise and I arranged a Bed and Breakfast in walking distance to the home the course was held in. It was always a delight to be in each others company for giggles and laughter were always on the menu.

I shan't bore you with the ins and the outs of the course, no I would rather concentrate on the one element that both surprised and puzzled me.

The course leader aka prestigious English Medium sat at the head of the circle and requested that I sit for Trance Healing with another student who I had just met. I did as I was bid.

I brought my chair into the centre of the circle and with the patient student sitting close to me. I began asking my guides to draw near. The other students were observing, I could hear them talking but was not aware of what was being said. I drifted into my trance state and was shown by my guides that healing would not take place at this time. It would seem that my patient had a hidden device and the battery and metal would not blend with the healing energy they wished to use.

My guides impressed upon me that the hearing was the issue and that some parts of the inner ear had been malformed with some important structures missing entirely. It was their wish to work with this person to try and remedy the situation with grafting from other parts of the body to bring about a reconstruction of a functioning inner ear.

Well as I came back from my trance state and my patient was awake (it seemed she too had been entranced for the spiritual healing evaluation) I met with the gaze of the group.

The course leader asked me what had I experienced. So I relayed in detail what had occurred. That the trance state achieved at this time was a spiritual consultation as to a healing session. I then, went on to explain what the Guides had told me with reference to the hidden metal and the issues within the inner ear. Bear in mind I was some what in awe of my fellow students and a little embarrassed that the task of Trance Healing did not take place.

The student that I was set to heal announced that she was wearing a small hearing aid and yes did confirm the issues with missing parts of the inner ear. There was much discussion as to what was being observed by the others in the group and it was agreed that another healing session would follow. This time without the hearing aid.

I don't normally have sweaty palms, but I did as I sat again with the same student as a patient. This was a big ask from the Spirit World and I did wonder was it my Psychic Ability that alerted me to her current hearing issues, was it my Ego that felt it could heal such a congenital issue. Yes I was a little wobbly. I surrendered to my Guides and Spiritual Team what will be will be.

As with every trance session I take a deep breath and on the exhale I let go and let God fill my space as I refill my lungs, and the exquisite addictive feeling of unconditional love did swirl and flood my whole being.

On awakening from this Trance session I awaited for several minutes for the patient to come around. She awoke slowly. All eyes on her, expectantly awaiting the outcome of this healing session.

She didn't say anything for a while. Eyes wide slow slim streams of tears fell from her eyes and she said she could hear the birds outside, it would seem that it did work.

Here is the thing, I am such a doubting Thomas, really I shouldn't be. But I am. After all the oohs and the ahhs and the proclamation that I should really push forward with my Trance healing blah blah blah. I just wasn't so convinced that the student was healed. It was a gnawing feeling and one I could not shake.

It would seem that my feelings on the matter were correct. The Student who I remained in contact with did speak with me again. It seemed it was a temporary fix and that her hearing, although, somewhat improved, she still needed the hearing aid. We were in different parts of the world and I offered to send distant healing.

It was not long after that course that Ciara a Northern Irish student came privately for a healing session. A cyst had been found on her brain. I sat a number of times with her in the Trance state with my Guides and

Healers working on her. By the time she saw her consultant for another scan there was no trace of the cyst.

My conclusion is that there may need more than one session to bring about the healing required for a condition in an individual. The individuals desire to be healed is also necessary.

Not all conditions can be cured!

23. MISSING PERSONS

2 September 2017

I am often called to help look for missing people. Only when it is a close family member, such as a sister, mother, father, etc., do I attend the meeting. I am deeply saddened by the number of requests I get to help find missing people. I am constantly contacted through social media to help find this person or that person with the words after, "It will make you famous if you find them," or "It will validate your work if you locate blah blah."

Although primarily, I hope these individuals are well-wishers, I reply that I only work with people who are directly family members of the missing person and that they are seeking my help, not the other way round with me reaching out to them.

Families of missing people go through so very much, and sadly, through social media, they are targeted by not-so-nice people at a time when they should be supported. It was only very recently that I received such a request to help find a missing woman.

The person who contacted me through Facebook Messenger said she desperately wanted to help the family. She didn't know them but really wanted to help. When I told her my method of operating, she thanked me.

I was then contacted by three different family members, cousins, who were told to contact me directly because I had leading information on the missing person case. Of course, this was untrue; I had no information at all.

A number of days later, I was contacted by the missing person's sister. She was a lovely lady. During the phone call, it was made apparent that someone had intimated that I had vital information and evidence of her missing sister and would only speak with a direct relative. She didn't understand why I wouldn't just go to the police.

I explained that I held no such information and that I was a psychic medium and that I only did this work when requested by a direct family member. I told her how sorry I was that this was happening and that in no way had I reached out to her, nor did I wish to cause her or her family more distress. She then told me of all the phone calls she was receiving, none of them helpful or supportive. It was such a terrible time for the family. She ended the conversation very politely by letting me know that she would never use a psychic medium and wished me a good day.

I would never push myself or my gift onto someone; I have a personal responsibility to those that are alive and to those that have crossed over. I will not just willy-nilly tune into that story or that person without their express permission.

Permission granted.

I was contacted by a young woman. Her brother had gone missing. Her parents were beside themselves with worry. No information was coming forward. It was as if he had just disappeared off the face of the earth. After chatting with the young lady, I agreed to meet her.

I met with my clients' two sisters. Once again, she reiterated that her brother was missing and, please, could I help? I was handed a three-dimensional jigsaw world globe that their brother made. No other information was forthcoming from my clients.

I lifted my heart to the spirit world and was saddened by the very quick reply from the client's brother. He had slipped and fallen into water and explained that his body would be found soon near a large drain. I knew he loved traveling and that he was in Australia.

My meeting gave an ease to the clients with her brother sharing many memories of fun times and, of course, his love and sadness that they didn't get to say goodbye. He reassured his sister that he was with his grandparents and would communicate again with the family when they got over the shock of his passing.

After such devastating news to deliver, the sisters thanked me and said they would keep in touch. I hugged them both. A week or two later, I received a text message. They said that his body had been found just as I had said, along with gratitude for my time and my gift.

One very different meeting was with a father. He had travelled from the south of Ireland, some two hours away, for this sitting. He held in his hand a photo of his daughter. I had a very uneasy feeling as I held the photo and looked at the image of the beautiful woman in the picture. He was telling me she had been missing for a number of weeks and just wanted to know if she was OK. The sitting felt off, wrong, and I grew increasingly uneasy. The daughter was indeed still alive and from spirit I was told to say nothing. I apologised to the man, saying how sorry I was, but I was unable to help other than to tell him that I did not sense her soul in the spirit world. He left quietly and calmly and thanked me for my time.

Two weeks later, a lady turned up for her appointment. She had a beautiful Southern Irish accent. On reading her, I realised she was the lady in the photograph. I knew she had run away from an abusive and controlling father and that she would move twice more before she felt safe.

Not all parents are nice, and not all children are grateful. Each person has their own story, and not all stories are happy.

24. A GHOST FROM MY PAST

October 2017

Never in a million years did I think that I would be meeting said course organiser again, who is now to be referred to as "Said Tutor." I had expertly avoided all levels of physical contact during his lifetime and it was a huge surprise coupled with other emotions such as shock mixed with horror as he stood in his perfect ethereal body beside one of my students at a Residential Spiritual Weekend I had organised and was tutoring with the aid of another assisting medium (who incidentally knew him well). And yet the meeting did take place, albeit from the world of spirit.

The residential I had organised was held in a beautiful Victorian Manor House which sat quite perfectly on the edge of a stunning golden beach, overlooked by the famous Musseden Temple in the small village of Castlerock Co Antrim, Northern Ireland. The furniture was sparse but adequate for our needs. Sleeping arrangements were in both dormitory and double rooms, all housed with period wrought iron beds tastefully covered with patchwork quilts and painted in mat national trust greens and blues. Soft chalky white wooden shutters adorned the massive picture windows and faded oriental rugs covered the dark wooden floors, adding to the charm of this once stately home. The house held an air of calm and peace and was obviously designed to ensure that every window had a view of that never-ending beach.

What joy. I had used this venue many times before, and memories of working with Denise flooded my mind as I looked around the house before the students arrived. We both had and felt quite at home in this space, and, yes, it was a little sad to be returning without her, but I knew in my heart she would be supporting me from heaven.

The students arrived from all over Ireland; some had travelled as far as Cork, a huge 8-hour drive, and if using public transport, the journey would be most certainly longer. Some of the students I had the pleasure of knowing through other courses I had taken, whilst others were just embarking on their spiritual pathway.

The oohs and ahhs were audible from the back kitchen as students displayed their excitement and pleasure at the raw beauty of their surroundings for the weekend. Squeals of delight and childlike mirth are my favourite sounds. In October, the Irish weather was kind, allowing students the added bonus of exploring the unspoilt beaches and neighbouring countryside, a little piece of heaven. What better to ignite the soul and raise the spirits than being in the heart of nature that expresses all the elements? A true delight that was indeed felt by all.

After a light supper, it was time to get to work. The first group session was about to start. All headed into the front parlour, where chairs had been placed in a circle, and quietly the students took their places.

Both myself and the assistant tutor sat with the whole group, as I normally start a weekend session with an open circle, a gathering of individuals wishing to develop their psychic abilities to blend with the spirit world.

In a residential setting, I have found it valuable to set the intentions of the students for the work ahead, and as such, it is an integral part of the bonding of students as well as the blending of soul energy of guides, helpers, and teachers from the Spirit world. It is an opportunity for students to become comfortable with one another's energy and, of course, the all-important work with spirit.

After opening in prayer and various psychic exercises, the students started to connect with the spirit world. One student in particular was of interest to me. I watched as she built her energy and raised her vibrations.

I became aware of a man standing directly behind her. At first, I didn't recognise this rather handsome man, but I was mesmerised and the apparition softly held my gaze.

It was only when the student medium began describing her communicator that I knew exactly who he was. Yes, it was said, tutor, aka, course organiser.

I moved further back in my chair and observed and listened, hoping the assistant tutor with me would recognise one of her mentors. Alas, she didn't. Nor was she aware of his actual presence in the room. It would seem I was the only witness to his presence, and I was more than just a little surprised and somewhat uncomfortable. The last time we met was rather unpleasant. And here he was communicating with one of my students. What was he going to reveal? My mind raced.

He stood tall without the aid of any sticks, his face perfect without sign of Bell's Palsy, and his hair dark and immaculate. A rather fetching man in all accounts, and most probably the spirit version of his younger years, there could be no doubt in my mind as to who he was.

The student began to express the communicator's "AKA Said Teachers" personality perfectly. There is no doubt he was helping, assisting, and coaching her. After all, he was an exceptional medium in his day.

I nudged the assistant tutor discreetly and, in a low tone, let her know who the communicator was and stated that the message was obviously for her as she had more dealings with the gentleman.

The message content was interesting. It was generally about now being the time to be centre stage, taking mediumship further afield to explore different countries and their cultures by travel and by using various means of communication as we have it today. Hmmm, it sounded familiar. The communicator mentioned a rather large fairy and as my accompanying tutor was same sex she readily acknowledged that information with a laugh saying she was "a big fairy". I dismissed that there could be any connection to me at all. I listened and thought, "Wow, what a fabulous message from spirit."

It wasn't until I returned to my room to structure my lesson plans for the next day that I noticed a tea towel (which I had not packed) with a huge fairy glaring at me from my case. It was the Cecilia Barker Christmas Tree Fairy Tea towel. Was the message for me? Was he really going to help me?! I sent a thought to Said Tutor and thanked him and asked for further signs that his message was for me and that all past issues had now been resolved. Should he wish to help, I would be more than willing to take assistance and guidance from him. No sooner had the thought been formed in my mind, a single white feather drifted peacefully in front of my face in an area where no feather could have come from. I smiled and inwardly said, OK, we will see.

My assistant tutor became sick the next day and, was rather too unwell to teach. Her group of students were small, and I absorbed them into my group, as home was really the place to be when ill.

I called upon the assistance of said tutor in the Spirit World and asked for some help. He had been a rather complicated soul in life, brilliant but complicated, well versed in all things mediumistically, and yes, he fought his own demons, as we all do in life. And here it was that another past tutor of mine wanted to work with me. Boy am I blessed.

The presence of Said Tutor has been felt quite often now as I lead my group in attuning to the spirit world. He was a huge advocate of sitting in the power, i.e., the power of your own soul. It has been this element that he has been working with me on, introducing new concepts and understanding of this great power we hold within us. As in life, he did make various CDs of his meditations, and this was something he urged me to do. OK, I said, I will when the timing is right.

25. THE SUMMONING FROM SPIRIT

December 2018

From time to time, I am summoned from the Spirit World. These visits happen rather randomly and when I least expect them, and in saying that, I will talk about one such event I recently had as I erected my rather large remote-controlled Christmas tree.

There I was, held in the delight of a heady dream of a hot sun, sand, and the soothing splish and splash of an azure-warm and gentle sea when a thought not of my own making came to life in my mind. What are you doing?

"I was doing ok," I said, slightly irritated by the intrusion of this thought and the now stark reality of winter with all its glory of dark, wet, and cold with lightning speed coming into focus as I opened my eyes, peering into the darkness under my warm snuggling duvet. "We have something to show you." The thought persisted.

I held my breath for a moment and thought about the statement I was about to make.

I could say I'm busy, I'm sleeping, I am enjoying my little sun experience. I thought I was allowed to sleep. It is where I find my creativity. And as I sank deeper under my duvet, I thought to myself, "It's my only day off, so I can be lazy." Oh yes, I had challenged the thought that had not yet entered my mind, and with that little act of defiance, I pulled the covers further up over my head.

A voice, not quite muffled but loud and clear enough, said, "Get Up." I drew back the cover to yell at the person being so rude, hoping it would be my husband, but knew he would be sleeping. Yes, soft sleepy snores emitted from the huddled shape beside me. It was dark in the room. That man sleeps through everything, I muttered.

OK, OK, I grumbled under my breath. I had been summoned by the spirit world, and now I am awake. The bedroom was very still. My two dogs lay undisturbed, totally unaware of my rude 5:30am awakening. The dogs stretched and yawned as I stepped over them.

"Really?" I said asked loud (my irritation was hard to hide) as I made my way to the bathroom. The tiles were so incredibly cold beneath my feet, it made me shiver. Boy, it's cold. I could see my own breath as I went about my ablutions. I closed my eyes as the warm water caressed my face and thoughts about the gentle sea returned. A disjointed voice from somewhere jolted me back with a loud 'Now ok, ok, I'm coming I returned to my bedroom to pull my woollen shawl around my shoulders.

I was definitely putting on the heating. As I made my way to the kitchen, two very excited dogs followed me, weaving in between my legs, nudging into my thighs. Hey girls, what's got into you both? As they jumped and circled me down the hallway. I opened the door that led to the kitchen, quickly flicked the already filled kettle on and checked the heating switch. I pushed the advance switch and the boiler groaned into action. Two excited dogs bounced and skipped with delight around the room. It was still very dark outside. In fact, I said out loud to my unseen visitor, "it's the middle of the night," knowing full well they would know my thoughts just as well as my spoken words. I opened the back door for my two now-hyperactive fur babies. What was this all about and on a Sunday morning at stupid o'clock? I do like my sleep, you see, and I am far from being a morning person! And to be honest, these impromptu visits from the spirit do unnerve me a little.

95

The coffee was hot, strong, and milky, just what one needs when you are awoken in such a strange manner. What was I doing? And more importantly, why was I doing it? My obviously very clever dogs made their way back to the bedroom, found their place and returned to their sleep state. I should join them, I thought as I secured the back door and walked into my conservatory, which housed my oversized all-singing, all-dancing Christmas tree, bought on a whim a number of years back, when my husband remarked that my then tree was too small, puny, and thin to be photographed and displayed on my Facebook page.

Well, you can't say that now, can you? I smiled as I flicked the switch to set the conservatory alight. Wow, that's pretty, I thought as the room glowed and danced with the multi-coloured twinkling lights enhanced by the contrasting darkness outside. The light reflection on the conservatory glass intensified and multiplied the experience. My house was asleep, and I and the Christmas tree where the only ones awake.

What was the urgency? I sipped my coffee and bathed in the light that surrounded me. I love Christmas, even the sad ones. They are all so very special and I do like twinkling fairy lights.

I threw my thoughts up to the spirit world and asked, "What am I doing and what am I missing?" There was no reply forthcoming and I started to drift in my mind to all the Christmas trees I had marvelled at and, indeed, every Christmas holiday I could remember.

I recalled my first Christmas. We had a silver tree decorated with multicolored lights. The ornaments were old 60's style glass shapes of vibrant reds, greens, and orange modestly distributed evenly on the shimmering silver branches. The presents beneath were carefully wrapped and box-shaped, all matching in colour and design, bar two large giraffe-shaped ones (I did love those presents; my twin and I called them Measles and Contagious).

I must have been three or maybe four years old. I felt the excitement of my younger self and the magic that surrounded me, and I held my breath when I saw my parents, both young and vibrant.

Oh my, they were a handsome and happy couple. Fat warm blobby tears splashed down my cheek, not of sadness nor of joy. I don't know what the emotion was, but it brought me back to my present waking moment. My coffee was cold. I quickly made another and returned to my seat. This was special, and I continued to remember.

The silver tree was a fabulous feature in my visits to Christmas. It held a power of its own, for from time to time it would radiate an electrical force field and discharge a shock to the inquisitive one who would squeeze or poke at the presents. A great deterrent, I might add, and one I had experienced firsthand. God, of course, is always watching.

Not all Christmases were happy, and as I grew older and realised that Santa was a mythical energy that touched the hearts and minds of adults to share in the gifts of the Christ Child, and if money was limited, this would reflect on the gifts received, I became more skeptical of Santa.

Readers of a certain age may well remember the delight of waking up to a sock filled with nuts and tangerines and perhaps a bag of shiny golden chocolate coins. I was of that generation, and finances became increasingly tight after my father's passing.

The first Christmas without him was hard and also lacked the presence of the much-loved silver Christmas tree. My mother did her best with the little money she had in a new house and a new county. The gifts were practical, and we all tried to appreciate them. I look back at that particular Christmas with a little shame at how my 11-year-old self-reacted to the new slippers and pyjamas, both one size bigger so I would grow into them, not to mention the apron! A requirement for home economics.

My teenage Christmases were not the happiest; they lacked the joy and magic I had felt as a child. Perhaps I was still grieving. I was quickly reminded of my first Christmas with my first born son. He was one year old, and my real Christmas tree was huge. All the ornaments were placed high up as my son, Jack, was an early walker and climber. I could actually smell the spruce tree. There we go, there was the joy and magic back in Christmas. I fell into the memory as easily as taking a breath. The very first ornament I bought for my son twinkled in front of me and lulled me back into the space of the young mother. I had been full of the wonder and joy of loving and giving.

I looked at my oversized Christmas tree and smiled. All my sons are adults now and a total humbugs when it comes to Christmas. A full cup of cold coffee greeted my lips. I don't mind cold coffee; it was one of the things I grew accustomed to when the kids were small. Three kids under the age of five is rather busy.

Eh up there we go, the sun had just started to break the night's sky. A new day was dawning, and I'd spent my early morning hours daydreaming in Christmas' past. What was I doing?

I watched the sunrise, unique and wonderful as the darkness was dispelled with a blaze of yellow, erupting into spectrums of red, orange, and purple. My description will never do it justice; it was just spectacular. I watched in awe, totally spellbound by the intensity of colour and light as the day grew and the darkness of the night sky faded into yesterday. I had one of those feelings of being an incredibly small part of something rather large. The beauty of nature moved me, and my soul shook with the excitement of having witnessed and been a part of something truly unique. I was wide awake and present, held in the still and quiet of the birth and beauty of a brand-new day.

A familiar feeling embraced me, coupled with a thought not of my own, and it did dance within my mind. Yes, it was the Spirit World.

"Leave the past behind, take forward only the joy and wisdom from your experiences, and greet this day as it has come to you, sweet and unused in splendour and in light."

It was rather a remarkable visit, a journey from Christmases past to the spectacular sunrise I witnessed. The words still resound in my mind.

I had been reminded that in life we have exceptional experiences, both happy and sad, both good and bad, all of which are indeed valuable and carry a wealth of knowledge. We can, at times, hold on to negative experiences. All of these slow our vibration down and hold us back in our soul growth. I was able at that time to release all sorrow and misgivings and marvel at the gift we receive each and every day, whether we witness the sun rise or not.

Each day is given to us fresh, pure, and beautiful, to create joy and to be joyful in our pursuits, be it work, family or indeed seasonal festivities. At the time, I did not realise that I harboured such feelings of hurt, shame, guilt, and a number of other darker emotions and to release these was a blessing, a huge healing and it left me as the day was birthing feeling free, humble, and privileged. I had been summoned at the crack of dawn for a huge healing session, and that was in itself just marvellous. No wonder it took the guts of four and a half hours to complete, and yet the time just whizzed by.

I was also gently reminded of the need for self-care. When one is in service, one does give and give and give. I was instructed to take time for me, to ensure that I was not being energetically pulled down by the sadness, or the anger, frustration, and pain from my clients. Boundaries were needed and time for me was now a thing.

26. STRANGE DREAM

May 2019

Bashing, pulling, and rearranging the pillows, I snuggled down and pulled my plump feather duvet up past my neck and under my chin. Thoughts of the day's events came into focus and dissolved into nothingness, whilst others required deeper probing. Those thoughts were challenged and put into specific categories. There had been one small thought that had the appearance of a worry. It was attached to work and I thought I would explore it more deeply.

I drifted into a sleep that was neither soft nor gentle. I was on a boat, or to be more precise, I was the boat. The water was moderately choppy, as if the storm was over but the water had yet to settle. I tasted the water. It was fresh with no trace of salt, and I smiled to myself that I was a boat with a mouth.

The sky was deep blue and clouds were forming. Strange how dreams are, they flit from one thing to the next and there I was speaking to people who I had never met before about the strange formation of the clouds and I said, "Quick, we need to take cover." They refused to listen and I ran to a doorway with a deep porch.

It started to hail first, with tiny white hard small balls, followed quickly by large chunks of ice. I picked one up and marvelled at the sheer size and weight of the lump of ice that filled the whole of my hand and realised that clumps of ice this size could do some serious damage. I could see there were already casualties from the falling ice rocks.

Then the sun danced across the porch and glistening puddles stretched for miles. The dangerous ice rocks had melted and the casualties were being attended to.

Beside me stood a man of colour in a white suit smoking a cigar, he reminded me of Morgan Freeman in the movie Bruce Almighty. He looked directly at me and said, "They don't know how to listen."

I read this now and think that this may have been a warning of what was to follow, the pandemic.

27. THE RELEVANCE OF WATER

January 2020

Tonight, I met a soul within my dream state. This was no ordinary dream. There was a lesson to be taught. I am no stranger to these experiences and have had many throughout my life. They take many forms, but tonight it would be with a Hooded Figure.

The dark, hooded figure was neither menacing nor overly friendly. There was a coolness to his frankness. I immediately sensed he was male. Communication between us was visual, with the odd outbreaks of auditory words encompassed by a vast range of human emotions.

This soul shared that he had taken the lives of many during his lifetime. It was a statement given without the weight of its truth attached. You would think I would have been scared to meet such a soul, but I was not. I was interested in what he had to say and what he had to show me.

I asked if he was happy. He said there is a need for water.

I asked if he was thirsty. He said there is no mouth nor tongue to quench

I asked what the relevance of water was.

He attempted to show me the meaning from the feeling of just walking down a dimly lit corridor. I was now in a large lobby with a majestic marble floor with veins of dark to light gray, muted browns, and rich, glittering gold beautifully threaded through the stark whiteness of this exquisite stone.

He stood tall in his dark robe; I could not see his face or gauge his age, his identity purposely hidden. It would seem from this experience that who he was in life was irrelevant.

He held a pure-yarn industrial mop with a wooden handle in his pale hand and a galvanised tin bucket by his feet. Both cleaning devices, I could tell, were brand new. There was no water in the bucket. The absorbent material fastened to the handle was soft, white, and dry as bone.

He pushed the mop against the floor, making it shine, but I instinctively knew his purpose was to lighten the darker veins within the floor. Miraculously, there was a small sprinkling of water on the dark vein of the marble. It glistened like liquid silver.

The man furiously mopped away at the dark tinges of the marble. When he finished, the dark tinges were significantly lighter. I knew that someone, in their fullness, had forgiven him for what he had done to them.

He explained that the floor looked remarkably different from when he first arrived, for it was more akin to black obsidian. It had taken years of individual forgiveness for his transgressions to transform the floor and, with it, his soul.

It was sensed that he still had a ways to go in the forgiveness area, as each dark streak was a pain he had inflicted on a person, felt, and remembered by family, friends, or colleagues. Each person he had affected was required to forgive him before he could be fully reunited with his loved ones.

I asked what it felt like when the water came (which I know was the symbol of forgiveness). He said it was like letting out a breath you had been holding for a long time. It was a good but sad feeling because he deeply and sincerely regretted injuring that person. He accepted the forgiveness with great reverence, for he acknowledged how difficult a journey it had been for an individual soul to come to that point of consciousness to let go of the pain he had caused. He was eternally grateful.

I pointed to the glistening gold veins on the marble floor and asked their meaning. He said not all my life on earth was wrong, and some of the gold you see was earned whilst here. They represent the good in my life and the honour of serving others unconditionally.

I looked around this vast lobby and could not see another soul. I asked if he was lonely. He said he was not, as others, such as himself, were waiting on forgiveness. I asked if they all had mops and buckets. He said each soul creates its own version of contrition, which is indeed a very private matter in terms of how it is expressed and rarely shared with others.

In answer to my next thought, he stated there was a common space should they wish to seek company or receive visits from loved ones. The shared space was comfortable and could accommodate all manner of visits. Within this space, there were opportunities for all who sought enlightenment and wished to seek company or receive visits from loved ones. Those who wished to share their story to facilitate learning with others were also encouraged.

I felt somewhat overwhelmed by the enormity of the concept I was being shown and knew there was so much more to what I was witnessing.

I said this was huge. Did you have to figure all this stuff out by yourself? Was there any guidance offered or given?

He stated that he would have other souls visit him in the shared space from time to time. Some were his family; others were more evolved beings that helped him to unpick the emotions and feelings attached to actions and non-actions throughout his life experience.

I asked him, "Is this heaven for you?" He said yes, pointed to a rather ornate art deco gold elevator, and said one day, when all had been forgiven, I will transcend to be forever with my loved ones.

I asked him what this space was called.

He said it was called HOPE.

28. THROUGH A NEW LENS

March 2020

I knew 2020 was a visionary year. I would hear myself quote the "2020 vision" and "how we would look at the new year through a new lens." That, eventually, we as a species would become more conscious of the needs of others and that a huge spiritual growth would follow. I did not know it would be in the form of a pandemic. Well, not entirely.

I don't watch the news as a rule, but at the end of January I was more concerned about the new virus that was emerging from China. So many horrible viruses have started there, like H5NI, aka Bird Flu. The SARS epidemic was also a coronavirus in late 2002 and 2003. Swine flu, another coronavirus, originated in Mexico in 1999, indicating that the problem is not limited to China. All of these were terrible, life-threatening diseases. So, a part of my mind felt it necessary to keep track of what was going on.

I launched myself into work with gusto, for 2020 was to be a busy year for me and January was to be fabulously busy with my Upfront and Personal tour kicking off with my special Psychic Tea Party in Antrim, workshops at the Psychic Studio, followed by tours in the north of Ireland: Portadown, Omagh, Derry and Ballymena. February was just as busy; Clogher, Larne, Eglinton, Belfast, Ballycastle, Portglenone,

Cookstown, Bangor demonstrations were all busy and all sold out with workshops filled to capacity. Yes, I was busy, but I was also very nervous. Kevin felt I was working too hard. I was not so sure. I had spoken to my friend in New York and told her that I didn't think the trip would go ahead. We had a few trips booked and had arranged demonstrations, workshops, and meet-ups with people, so she said let's wait until we are sure before we cancel. The virus had reached the shores of Ireland on the 29th of February and this was about to change everyone and everything.

I was watching Italy and how the spread of the virus was affecting the country. March was to be a very busy month with travel planned to New York on the 18th of March, in May I was to be in Slovenia, June, Amsterdam, and I had to fit Spain in somewhere. My diary was bulging.

I was in the south of Ireland on the 9th of March, Dundalk to be precise. I was becoming more uncertain and worried. I was in a beautiful hotel, and the demonstration was going well. A lady sneezed and coughed loudly in the audience. It seemed like everyone stopped and stared at her. I made a joke and carried on, but a huge shiver of fear rippled down my spine. I finished the demonstration and told Kevin this was the last physical live demonstration with my asthma. I couldn't risk it. I was going online for now. The virus was coming and we needed to prepare.

I was not wrong, a bit annoyed by the "Don't worry, you're going to be OK" advice from above. They could have expanded on that for me. I was without doubt frightened. America was looming and I had contacted my friend in New York and told her I doubted if I would be flying. Yes, everything looked OK; flights were flying; business as usual for the rest of the world. I told her that we would wait and see but to prepare for what was coming. So, within a few weeks, New York became the new epicentre of the virus. Flights were compromised. The travel bans from Europe to the United States came into force on the 14th of March, with the UK and Ireland following quickly on its heels.

I began contacting the venues I had booked to reschedule events and cancel others, knowing that time was of the essence and that it would not be long before all hotels would be closed. I had just finished my last call on the 18th of March, and by the 20th, hotels were all closed.

My private sittings filled my days, which incidentally were all online. Some readings showed the pain and anguish which was to come. This gave me a deeper insight as to what was going on and I prayed silently to myself. Northern Ireland officially went into lockdown.

29. FOR WE ARE ALL
APART OF THE GREAT WHOLE

March 2020

The Wuhan Flu, novel Coronavirus, COVID-19, "the thingy," broke out in November 2019 and quickly spread throughout its Provence. Flights were still leaving for other countries, bringing the deadly virus to other shores. It was alarming how fast it hit a country, bringing it to its knees in a matter of months. Borders were closed, the country was on in lockdown, and flights were stopped. As I write, Italy is on lockdown, and it is unavoidable that the United Kingdom and Ireland will follow suit. I do feel the worry and the fear that comes with every news bulletin.

I was asked at the beginning of March if we should be worried. I replied, "No." Shopping has been strange; shelves are empty and items are being rationed. Soap and hand sanitisers are hard to get. I made just over two litres of hand wash last January at a spiritual retreat and wondered then how I would use it. I stored it in jars in the office, and it certainly has come in handy.

I have changed my working habits, reducing the level of physical contact as advised by the World Health Organisation. Hugging and hand-holding my clients is now a thing of the past. As nobody wishes to breach the two-meter personal space requirement to reduce the spread of the virus. From my readings, I am seeing how this virus will affect families, and it is sad.

For once, my asthma has settled and the need to use my reliever has lessened. China says it is in recovery but I am not so sure, the USA has flight restrictions on Europe.

I throw my consciousness up to the spirit world and their essences comfort me. Normally, countries are suspicious of one another, and governments bicker and point fingers in an accusatory manner. However, we are now seeing people put aside their pettiness, roll up their sleeves, and cooperate in ways that humans require. This virus is non-discriminant and will sweep the world, taking with it both the sweet and the sour.

My self-isolation began on March 18th, 2020, as in, that was the last day I was out of the house. I am a brittle asthmatic, and my nephew, who is staying with me and my family, has cystic fibrosis. We both need to be shielded.

I remember my last day out as if it was yesterday. I had already started to self-isolate a number of days before, but it was essential that I go to the bank that day. I knew that within weeks, everything would be contactless as cash could carry the virus.

I had finished my banking and was about to leave the building when a lovely lady called my name. She flung her arms around me. She was delighted to see me. She was such a kind lady who told me how she followed me on Facebook and thought the world of me as she had been lucky enough to receive two free readings with me on Facebook. We chatted for a while, and she again hugged me and thanked me for the messages from spirit that I had given her. Kevin looked at me sideways and made a face; the plan had been for minimal contact and social distancing, but that was not to be the case; everywhere I went that day, people wanted to hug me.

At home and in lock down with three teenage lads, it has been more challenging for the boys than me. I have explored YouTube and found it to be rather amazing. There are many free courses to choose from; one in particular, I might add, ballet, left me crippled for a number of days.

I have been blessed to be able to work from home and enjoy the gift of technology that gives me the window from my home to yours, a new way of working virtually, safe, and still upfront and personal.

It has been working with spirit that has kept me sane. It has been that closeness to my spirit guides that has kept me grounded. But I must admit I know that this experience will affect me.

30. FEAR CAN BE TRICKY

April 2020

Most people are so riddled with fear that they don't even recognise when the emotion has overtaken their lives. Because fear can be tricky like that.

Fear was never really a thing for me. Sure, I got scared from time to time, but fear was something I never really experienced until I did. And when I realised what it was, it had a grip on me. I personally believe that everything we experience has a reason. It's a test, a challenge to open our hearts to be more compassionate, understanding, and loving. To understand oneself and promote personal growth.

Think of your life, every act you engage in, every decision you make comes out of two different emotions or states of being. Fear or love.

It is a simple, straightforward, and often overlooked fact: the opposite of love is not hate. The opposite of love is fear.

I remember back to October 2019, in my home office in Randalstown where I had been reading for my clients and, after say four days of seeing the same signs, woes, troubles, and disruption, I turned to my husband and said, "I think there is something wrong with me." I think

I have turned into one of those readers who is purely negative and only sees the worst possible outcomes."

He said simply (wise old Kevin), "Start looking for something else."

And you know what? He was right, we find what we look for. So, I started to look for the joy. Joy, and love, and laughter could be found dotted among the despair and fear that was largely being presented.

I strived to find the light in my readings, but I will be honest, I found it hard. By the end of October, I knew there would be a world event; I just didn't know what it was. My spirit guides told me all would be OK and I had nothing to worry about. All would be good and as it should be. I would be protected. I would be provided for. I was not to worry but to follow their lead. I was to trust.

I had a residential in January 2020 where we all made natural soap, liquid soap, and facial scrubs free from parabens with natural ingredients and essential oils. I came home from that workshop with three litres of liquid soap.

"When will we ever use that amount, my husband asked?" Needless to say, it came in handy because you could not buy liquid soap for love nor money, just a few short weeks later, and we sure did all smell lovely during lockdown.

Led by my guides, they had me organising back-to-back demonstrations in January, February and right up until the 9th of March, my last demonstration by choice. By then, everyone knew what was coming.

My friends in New York, Italy, Spain, Norway, Slovenia, and Australia kept me abreast of how things were in their countries and what was really happening. My work planned for these destinations, of course, was cancelled.

We lost loved ones to the thing. We did online funerals; it was a thing.

I stopped listening to the news. As the world went within.

I didn't leave the house; I rarely went out for a walk. Everything that came into the house was washed. I didn't sleep. I was highly strung. The only time I didn't feel like that was when I was working. So, I just worked and I didn't stop.

Fear was a thing with me and I had to learn to get rid of it. And it wasn't easy.

Anxiety and Panic Attacks I don't think I need to describe them to you; I can see you nodding as you read this paragraph.

Agoraphobia - to name but a few phobias I was developing at an exponential rate.

I remember having to go to A&E because I had a severe asthma attack. The doctors had phoned the hospital, and they were expecting me. I was ushered into a cubicle; my vitals were taken and back-to-back nebulisation with all sorts of solutions began.

The nurse popped the solutions into the equipment and left me. I could hear that the woman in the cubical next to me had tested positive. She was 84 and the gentleman, 56, was presenting with symptoms.

A young, handsome doctor came in. He pulled down his mask and flashed a smile, saying, "Fiona, are you worried about COVID-19?"

Despite being handsome, I replied, "Am I worried, I'm FAT, over fifty, and asthmatic. What do you think?"

"Oh, you miss understood me. Do you think you have it?" he asked.

I said no and he went on to say that I was rather poorly and needed to stay in hospital as my asthma was very brittle. I stopped him there and said, "Thank you for the invite, but no."

I would rather he gave me medication and I would be on my way. I wasn't for staying, there would be too many germs, and I left with a bag of medication to treat myself at home. Praying that I hadn't picked up the virus in the hospital.

31. WITH A CLEAR, PURE LIGHT

Spring 2020

Jesus Bids Us Shine with a Clear, Pure Light

Susan Bogert Warner (1819-1885)

I awoke to this song quietly playing at the back of my mind. A memory leapt forward in technicolour of my mum singing this to me. I was very young; it was nighttime and I was frightened. It always reassured me then that in the dark, my light could be seen, I was not alone, that my wee soul was shining just as brightly as the huge celestial bodies glow in the night sky, and my soul emanation was being carefully and lovingly monitored.

I know that my people upstairs brought this to my attention for a reason, so.

I'm a "Googler." I looked up the children's hymn and found the author. It was written in 1864 by Susan B. Warner, an American author better known for her book The Wide, Wide World, under the pseudonym Elizabeth Wetherell. But what prompted her to write this beautiful hymn?

From 1863 to 1875, the fourth pandemic of the 19th century swept away many lives. It was cholera. Quick on its heels was influenza. Had she been moved by the loss of life that swept away the young and old alike?

As the world closes its front doors and hunkers down, we are now literally in our own corner, and it would seem that we have been plunged into darkness with the pandemic we are currently experiencing.

I am drawn to the light that I see on social media. Caremongering as opposed to scaremongering. Acts of kindness, both small and large

The message from upstairs is clearly... Remember, you are not alone.

On the 26th of March, I held my first online Psychic Zoom Demonstration and I loved it. It was upfront and personal, with everyone attending getting a personal message from a loved one from above. Yes, there were learning curves, but I was no stranger to working online, having worked for the SNUI virtually for the last number of years. However, technology today is far superior.

My twin sister is a mental health nurse. She was redeployed to set up COVID hospitals and also to work within them. She gladly up-skilled to do her bit to combat the disease. Her son has cystic fibrosis. After taking him to her on the 10th of March, it was agreed that he would be better off staying with me, so we packed him up and took him to live with me in Randalstown for however long the duration of COVID-19 would be.

The loss via COVID-19 came early and I attended with great sadness my first online funeral in April. The death of a dear uncle in May triggered trauma from my past in a way which I did not expect nor understand. The need to be with my cousins and my family was so great and yet so hard. I was not able to attend and my asthma was being difficult. No, I will be honest I was frightened to go outside. There I said it, and it is true, I was petrified of being with people.

32. FROM A WINDOW ABOVE

May 2020

"Looking from a window above is like a story of love. Can you hear me?"

- Only You - Cover by Alison Moyet (back in my day.)

I was demonstrating on Zoom in what was becoming my usual Psychic Fiona's Special Saturday Online demonstration. I could see all the windows into the homes of those attending this unique and extraordinary event.

The spirit world often let me hear songs, and "Looking from a Window Above" played long and loud in my head from 6:15pm until 7pm.

When I opened up the Zoom meeting, there before me were all the windows of participants in the meeting eager to hear from spirit. The presence of a young male was close and strong.

He urged me to pick up a gladioli flower because it had significance. It's an exotic flower from a hot country. I usually associate it with Australia, but the song Viva Espana started playing within my mind and I accepted the geographical connection and it was understood.

The young man in spirit was reaching out to his mother, oddly enough. "The Window Above my image," he had been a DJ, so the message was through songs, which she understood fully.

The message was tender, full of love and acceptance as his body had been repatriated not that long ago. He had only passed away five months ago. He was appreciative of the Kevin Bell Foundation and wished so very much to be remembered with love by his sisters.

He ended with the song, Celine Dion's "My Heart Will Go On," and I must admit I was indeed teary-eyed for his mum, who understood and verified that she had been seeing him in her dreams.

Of course, I didn't sing it, because my voice doesn't work like that, but I knew the message was understood. My Zoom demonstrations were all very interesting, never two the same.

33. SLUGS IN THE GARDEN

May 2022

Growing tomatoes and vegetables in the garden are my husband's joy. We have had all manners of fruits and legumes flourishing in pots, planters and in the greenhouse. Fenced-in, private and secure, I feel safe sitting in the heart of this little oasis.

The lack of Aeroplanes in the sky has given nature a necessary break. As a result, there is a boldness to wildlife. I have seen foxes, hares, badgers, and daring birds who swoop arrogantly to nosh on the ripe red currant bushes. They do not fly away even when the dogs bark at them for trespassing; they barely lift their little birdy heads to acknowledge Bella and Lou Lou.

Gifted with green fingers, Kevin has grown a bounty of crops. There is nothing like eating homegrown fresh veg. But it is not without hard work.

Kevin removes the slugs from the planters each night and re-homes them elsewhere. He firmly believes that all, even the slugs, have the right to life. It is a battle, he tells me, as the little critters make their way back to the lettuces and beans no matter how far he relocates them.

I have been thinking about nature and power animals, and it got me thinking about the tenacity of the little slug.

Firstly not a creature of beauty, or are they? The soft, moist boneless body wears its slime on the outside, unlike us humans who wear it on the inside.   This silver secretion protects them as they move. Slugs could crawl over a sharp razor blade and not cut themselves. This creature has an oral cavity that contains at least 3000 razor-sharp teeth and two noses, one at the head and the other at the tail. Their sense of smell is powerful, which gets them around, like their internal sat-nav.

Hermaphroditic, the slug holds both the divine masculine and the divine feminine. If you are part of the LGBTQ+ community, the slug spirit animal (technically a mollusc) is here to encourage you to be yourself.

The slug has strength and can mate with any slug to create hundreds of little slug babies, and if needed, they can fertilise their own eggs, too, thus representing fertility and versatility.

So the slug's positive message would be to love yourself as you are, speak your truth and go at your god-given speed, for there is a silver lining wherever you may go. Fertility and creativity are in abundance.

The negative aspect of the slug would be that they need a backbone suggesting a lacking of courage. Slugs generally have not evolved nor changed dramatically from the Jurassic period meaning a rigidity of thought and barrier to change. Not the fastest of creatures could suggest laziness.

How interesting this little beastie is. I should look at other little creatures and make a collection of my thoughts me thinks!

34. CANCELLED FLIGHTS

May 2020

As the email for my Slovenia trips confirms the cancellation for all flights, I acknowledge the process to request a refund. It is with deep regret that I cannot go, for it is a trip to see a family I hold dear and share stories with. I grew to love this family in such a short time, and I FaceTime'd my friend. We had planned so many wonderful workshops and demonstrations. We had cancelled all the events a number of weeks ago, but it sure did bring memories of my first trip back in abundance of the joy I had there.

My first trip to Slovenia was in April 2019. My day started at stupid o'clock as my flight from Belfast was at 5:35am, the first flight to Stansted, with a connecting flight to Slovenia at 1:05pm. My asthma had been troubling me and I was on yet another course of steroids, so sleep evaded me for fear of, one, not breathing and two, missing my flight. The flights themselves were on time and super-efficient. Being dyslexic and extremely tired, I was fortunate to find myself with a lovely couple traveling to Slovenia, so like a little sheep, I followed them on to the train that would take us to Gate 19 and to my final destination, Ljubljana. I am always so fortunate when travelling. There is always assistance at hand, the Angelic Traveller, who is just there waiting to help me. Feeling so blessed.

Tadjea, my host, was waiting for me at arrivals and I drank in the beautiful snow-capped mountains. The time was now 4:10pm. Time-travelling again, Slovenia is one hour ahead of Northern Ireland. A quick stop to the shops to pick up gifts for her children, flowers for her mum, and a rather nice bottle of cognac for her dad. She informs me that they all live together in one big house.

She and her family live in a 3-block apartment built some time ago by her father for the family. The spacious apartments sit one on top of the other on a rather large garden plot encompassing the very important vegetable patch with a coveted polytunnel (always wanted one of those). A huge outdoor space with swings and a barbecue area and, in the summer months, a swimming pool; not too shabby a set up at all.

Tadjea's fresh wild mushroom soup, personally foraged by Tadjea's mum from local forests, was ready to sip, mopped up by freshly baked bread and followed by Mathew's famous apple strudel and served by Tadjea. After munching on gourmet-level cuisine, we made our way down to meet the parents. At this stage, I had been awake for eighteen hours.

I met Mathew and Yelka (Tadjea's Mum and Dad), a rather warm and fun-loving couple who were eager to share their stories of Ireland when they visited. Over red wine from a local vineyard (rather nice, I must admit) were plated traditional meats, sausages, salamis, and something that I needed to spit out, but according to Mathew, it held medicinal qualities to keep one regular. I don't believe he was offended, but I must add that it was rather disgusting (speh).

One last treat before bed, a meaty spicy pate on toast, which was delicious, and I demolished it off with a cup of ginger and lemon tea. The pate is called Biftek Tatarski Arvaj. A delicacy in Slovenia is made from raw meat and spices. I was glad Tadjea told me how it was processed after I ate it, but I must say it was rather yummy, so it is on my shopping list to take back home to let the boys and Kevin taste it.

I awoke as usual at stupid o'clock every morning in Slovenia at 5 past the hour of 5 in the morning (my body clock time was 6:05am). Every morning I take my tablets and medications with orange tea, which is rather refreshing. Tea is not my thing; I'm more of a coffee girl. However, I am starting to get into all these different flavoured teas. I listen to the dawn chorus and watch the sun rise from the balcony. Loving life. Making a lasting memory.

Slovenia, without doubt, is a rather beautiful country steeped in history, as you would imagine. My clients were lovely. My appreciation for salami and savoury sausages became a thing! Each client letting me know that they understood my liking for the spicy sausages came bearing gifts. So much so that I had to send, by post, a huge box containing all the sausages and other gifts my clients brought me. In all honesty, I could have set up a shop.

The workshops had been fabulous, the readings insightful, every day a new activity and the sightseeing incredible. For sure, long-lasting friendships were made. On my last day, I sat with Yelka, and I was more than teary-eyed to leave a family I felt so much for.

I won't go into detail about the cancellation of my other flights. Some operators did not understand the appropriate refund practices. Despite some difficulty, that was eventually resolved with an apology. As I filled in the form to recover funds, I recalled with great fondness my first trip to Slovenia, and I know the next couple of years to come will be better; more memories to make, more spicy sausages to eat. The sparkly earrings I bought at the airport adorn my ears at every workshop and demonstration now (seriously stupid price) and will always remind me of my very special Slovenian family.

35. THE NEW NORMAL

July 2021

I had been told by Upstairs I would be OK by April 2021, and yes, my jab of Pfizer had been administered on the 4th of April. It wouldn't stop me getting the thingy, but it would help me fight it off better if I did.

It was a dark time, and it certainly marked me. I became frightened. I didn't like going out or being with people. I was scared. The transition from lock down to back to normal was not easy either.

I remember my first demonstration. It was on the 1st of July 2021, locally in Toomebridge. Of course, it was sold out. Socially distanced chairs, facemasks, and hand sanitiser, all the usual suspects with track & trace. I was terrified of being in a room with so many people. The spirit world insisted I do it, and I did, and with each demonstration thereafter, my fear decreased (mostly because I got my 3rd booster jab and kept my distance).

Demonstrations during the lifting of restrictions have been a juggling act. Vaccine passports, lateral flow tests, and antibody letters are required for entry to any public place. The rules varied from week to week, and I likened them to the Hokie Pokie. At times, the requirements changed illogically.

My first demonstration was sold out in minutes of launching it to social media. Capping the numbers and insisting on the one-meter chair spacing rule kept me legally right. I mentioned I was terrified, and the truth of it all is that I was. Lockdown has altered me. It had made me fearful. I hadn't driven a car for 18 months.

Oh, that was a big fat lie. It was the month of May during the first initial lockdown. I took the keys and jumped into my car. The roads were empty and scary. I was halfway down the motorway when I realised I was heading to Bangor. I could go see my mum through the window, but that was all. I know she would have opened the door and I would have gone in. Yes, I would have broken the rules.

However, I could never forgive myself if I gave her the illness. You see, the teenage boys in my house were far from self-isolating. Their mental health was all over the place, and it was a living nightmare. I turned the car around and headed home, sobbing with big fat wobbly tears drenching my face. The enormity of the situation, huge, unsurmountable, and too much for me to bear. I arrived home promptly and went to bed.

It was with this memory in mind, I gently opened up my demonstration.

There I was stood in front of my audience in Toome, and the most incredible sense of spirit surrounded me, lifted me, held me, comforted, and encouraged me. It was just like the first public demonstration I did back in the day. I was in a space held with unconditional love. The audience's loved ones' stories were told. Laughter with tears was the overall emotion as mothers, sons, and lovers were reunited.

The nature of demonstrations has never altered in that it is an event where a psychic medium stands in front of a group of people, usually on stage, to randomly perform short (three to ten minute) readings for a few of the audience members.

The purpose of a public demonstration of mediumship is not to give everyone in the audience a reading. No, that is what many attendees hope for when attending a psychic medium demonstration, but this is not a forum for private readings. Yes, I may have some upfront and personal moments, but private readings are held in private without an audience.

It is the medium's desire that these demonstrations open people's minds to the possibility that an afterlife exists and that spirit communication is achievable. It is hoped that this will alleviate the fear of death, for in my mind, you can't die for trying. There is no death; life moves on in a different way.

There are those within the audience that are merely a plus one. There is no reason as to why they are there.

There are some that view a demonstration as a "wee night out," a bit of entertainment and they have a few drinks and at times can be tad disrespectful or in one case so disruptive that the police are called (that was Armagh a night hard to forget).

The majority, however, desperately want to connect with someone they have lost.

36. SPIRIT VOICES LOUD AND CLEAR

ITC PHENOMENA

February 2021

What exactly is ITC? ITC is an abbreviation for the term "Instrumental Trans-Communication". The term describes communication with non-physical entities through electronic devices.

Almost every electronic device in use today has been used to receive and record sounds, texts, and pictures.

On a live feed in February 2021, my iPhone activated Siri and said, "I am happy to be here." I glanced over to where the voice was coming from, and I became aware of a young man. I knew he hadn't connected to anyone on my live feed. He put his head to the side and smiled. I just laughed and said that would be the spirit world. It was about 15 minutes into the live feed.

I had a reading booked straight after my Facebook live. I had just finished and was preparing for my video call when again the device stated, "I am happy to be here."

The young man in spirit was waiting patiently. I was super excited to do the reading. I knew it was going to be amazing. It was one of those whoop whoop moments.

My 8:30pm appointment texted to reschedule their appointment to next week. I thought to myself, seriously, what am I going to do with the spirit person in the corner? I looked over at the young man with his broad grin, and he winked at me.

Within five minutes, I had been contacted by another person requesting a video reading. I offered them the cancellation and they took it. Wow, I thought to myself, the spirit world really knows their stuff.

My client was a young woman, and my spirit visitor was her brother. Of course, it was a joyful reunion full of evidence and shared memories. But the purpose of this journal entry is to recognise the element of ITC in daily life.

The spirit world interacts with us in so many ways. The signs are there, you just need to notice them.

I do find that spirit is interacting with my devices more and more. It is not uncommon for them to go off during my online video readings, playing songs that for the recipient are a validation that their loved ones are nearby.

Sometimes, and to Kevin's dismay, Alexa announces "we are here" at 3am. It's hard not to notice Alexa's booming voice in the bedroom, let alone the chill that goes down your spine when unexpected spirit people turn up. What did I do in that instance? I went back to sleep. I had to be up early as I had a hospital clinic to attend in Belfast.

Early the next morning, Kevin was driving me to the appointment when his dad popped into my head to say hello. It was his dad's birthday, and he wanted to let Kevin know that Robert was within and all was well. Ta ta for now, he said, as he left my mind.

Kevin was surprised with the message and said that the only Robert he knew was his cousin, and by all accounts, believed he was alive and well. However, he would check with the family when we got home. Kevin looked up his cousins on Facebook to find out what had happened to Robert. What sad news. Robert had indeed crossed over a number of weeks ago. Communication in families at times is not great. Luckily for Kevin, his dad in spirit let him know what was going on. Thank you, Gordon.

I have had countless experiences with ITC, all evidential and at times very insightful and helpful. If your Alexa, Google, or Siri is activated via mysterious means, it could very well be that you too are getting messages from a loved one.

37. BRIEF ENCOUNTERS WITH LASTING EFFECTS

12th, January 2022

The story takes place in a supermarket in New Jersey on Valentine's Day, February 14th, 2021. Michael Perino, a professor of corporate and securities law and author, tweets his story:

"At the supermarket today, I found a small, elderly woman standing in front of a high shelf holding @BonneMamanUS preserves. She was having trouble finding the flavour she wanted because the jars were set back on the shelf. She couldn't read the labels. She could barely reach them. I offered to help. After I handed her the raspberry preserves, she thanked me, paused, and then asked, "Do you know why I buy this brand?"

I laughed and replied, "Because it tastes good?"

"Yes, it tastes good." She paused again. "I am a Holocaust survivor."

This was not the conversation I expected on a Sunday grocery run.

"During the war, the family that owns the company hid my family in Paris. So now I always buy it. And whenever I go to the store, my grandkids remind me, 'Bubbe, don't forget to buy the jelly.'"

I told her that that was the best reason I ever heard to buy any company's product. And then we both smiled behind our masks and went our separate ways."

You can imagine how the Twitterverse reacted and how people began to comment and investigate the story. I must admit I did too. I visited the Holocaust Memorial Museum in Washington on the 14th of August 2019 and was very fortunate to meet Harry Markowicz, a Holocaust survivor who volunteered at the museum. He was an exceptional man. I remember the day so vividly.

The Holocaust Memorial Museum was must-see. I knew it would not be easy, nor would it be pleasant, but I was compelled to go, and Claire, my companion, agreed. Our time in Washington was limited and I was forever being told off for chatting to strangers. I know Claire would correct me and say, "Old men!" But our schedule was tight and she was right to chastise.

We entered the museum, and Claire went to the admission ticket desk. There was a queue and I just stood looking around the huge, vast entrance space in total awe of the building.

A woman approached me and said, "Look, there are a couple of men you need to talk to; they are survivors." I looked over at the two desks that were pushed together, dwarfed, in a corner of the vast lobby. I looked over at Claire in line and figured I had a few minutes before I was told off for chatting again.

Harry Markowicz wore a fine brown suit and a kind smile. He had twinkly eyes, full of life and mirth. I introduced myself. He pushed an A4 page towards me. It held his story. The man beside him, not so warm, pushed his page towards me. I thanked them both. The stories of both men were harrowing, hidden from the world to keep themselves safe.

Imagine folks telling your sad story over and over again. Why wouldn't it just drive you mad and depress you?

I asked Harry what he did when he wasn't at the museum, and we struck up a warm and humorous conversation. We were still chatting as Harry was telling me about his fond memories of his uncle, who was a cantor in Belfast, when Claire arrived beside me. She quickly caught on that these were no ordinary old men I was chatting to and gave me the look.

I said how sorry I was, but time was pressing and I had to get a move on as we were set to leave DC at 4:30pm.

The museum was designed in such a way that you went in one way and could only come out one way. There would be no turning back. It just couldn't happen.

I know because both Claire and I tried to find a way out to cut the exhibition short as the truth of the full horror in technicolour was so over powering. Six million men, women, and children were callously murdered by the Nazis in one of the most infamous genocides in modern history. The exhibition did not hold back.

We were committed to seeing the whole presentation. We could see the exit in sight, which brought us to the large lobby once again. I could see Harry with a swarm of people eager to hear his story. I don't know how he noticed me, but as we were leaving, he stood up from the crowd, waved and called "see you later, Belfast," and I waved back.

Claire and I thought we would never feel happy again after that exhibition. I suggested eating chocolate. That was Harry Potter's go-to after a Dementor attack.

The experience at the museum was profound, and it took several days before either of us felt right.

My demonstration is planned in Belfast on Friday, January 27, 2022, which happens to be the anniversary of the liberation of Auschwitz-Birkenau, now known as International Holocaust Remembrance

I didn't realise this date was special until I had a spirit visit to one of my dreams. It was Harry Markowicz. He told me in the dream that he enjoyed our conversation immensely. He delighted in my humour and wished me every happiness. I knew in my dream he had crossed over because he looked so good, so free, and happy. He said, "I'll be seeing you, Belfast." He waved and he was gone. I woke at 5:13am and I googled Harry, and there you have it, he had passed four months ago.

It was January the twelfth, 2022, at 5:13am. I found out that Harry had passed to spirit on the 15th of September 2020. He was an exceptional man, kind and extremely funny. Harry Markowicz I will always remember you as a bright light in a dark space.

On Thursday, the 27th of January, I opened my demonstration as a tribute to a fine, honourable man who had been a survivor. I talked about our meeting, and I must admit there were tears in my eyes. Such a brief encounter, perhaps fifteen minutes tops, with such lasting effects. I feel blessed to have met you, Harry, keep in touch.

38. MY DAISY

Daisy, a cross between a border collie and an Afghan hound, came into my life way before Kevin and the boys. She was rescued from Crawfordsburn Country Park on an icy cold, snowy day. I was working part-time in the Country Park at the front desk, taking enquires and bookings. Reports of a skittish-timed dog wandering the park for the last few days came pouring in. I alerted the wardens who would take care of such things. Dogs were not always reported; streakers and flashers were more the norm. But the wardens were quick off the mark and searched for the dog but could not find her.

Being in the visitor centre behind a desk that bitter afternoon, I saw the daisy bush by the window move in a way that I knew was not normal. On investigation, I saw the dog shivering inside the bush full of the dead-headed daisy flowers and bare twigs that had once been so vibrant in the summer.

I popped across the room to the restaurant. It was about 4pm and trade had been slow that day. No one really wanted to walk about in that weather, and it was getting darker fast. I was given four cooked sausages and I went out to the bush where the dog was hiding. Small flecks of snow were falling from a dark and heavy sky.

I tentatively threw the sausages into the bush and watched the dog sniff them and gobble them down. We had eye contact, and I threw the other sausages in half by half until this beautiful animal came close enough to put a little rope around her neck that the wardens had left (just in case).

She followed me into the warmth of the visitor centre and sat quietly at my feet. I called the relevant services, who informed me there would be no-one available that evening, so I let them know I would take her home. It was snowing after all.

After two weeks, no one was looking for her.

I took her to the vet, a lovely lady called Glenda, who was soon to be a friend. She checked her over and said she was fine I ordered her shots and signed up for a vet plan. I called the police and let them know the dog was with me should anyone have enquired. But no one did, and the police said, "it looks like you have a dog now, Fiona."

Daisy was black and tan with bright intelligent brown eyes like licked brandy ball sweets, and her nature was loving, soft, and gentle. Just what I needed at that time in my life with a horrid break down of a recent relationship. She was the loyal friend and companion I needed, and I thanked the heavens that I found her that day.

My new love, Daisy, accompanied me everywhere I went. She soon became a valued and loved family member. All my siblings doted on her. She was such a gem.

When dating, if Daisy didn't like them, I didn't date them. It's as simple as that. On the other hand, she loved and showed great affection for Kevin from the get-go. It was a sign!

I was somewhat worried when Jack was born about how she would take to babies. She had never been around them as far as I knew. But I need not be worried. Picture Nana from Peter Pan and there you have my Daisy.

Seventeen years I had that wonderful creature in my life. I remember saying to Glenda, the vet, "How will I know when it is time?"

Daisy had cancer in her eye and needed it to be removed, and I was so worried. Glenda told me that one day I would know, Daisy would tell me. I looked at my fur baby, a trusted and loyal companion, and hoped that day was far from now.

Daisy moved with us to Randalstown, and she enjoyed the countryside with Henry, our neighbour's dog, and Paddy, a black Labrador. They would walk together on the lane, but never far from the house.

She would sit with me in my caravan when conducting readings. All my clients loved her. She sat in workshops, and all my students adored her.

Daisy was ill. One day, as she lay on her orthopaedic bed beside mine in the bedroom, she let me know she was done and needed to go home.

I was so calm that day, so cool and organised. The boys got to say their goodbyes, and she kissed all three, too weak to stand for any length of time. I took her to the local vet who had been looking after her for the last few months, and they too were surprised at her demise.

Kevin carried her in and placed her on a soft blanket on the vet's table. She looked at me with her soft eyes, filled with gratitude. The injection had been given and Daisy closed her eyes.

Up until that point, I had been calm and collected. But this horrible noise erupted and hurt my ears. I didn't realise that the wail was coming from me. The howl came from deep within my soul and Kevin hugged me close.

I looked over his shoulder and my maternal grandfather stood with a young and happy Daisy, all ready to go, her tail with its white tip flicking left and right in exuberance.

Daisy had gone.

And, I was lost.

The mutual love and comradeship I have had the privilege of experiencing in this life is forever etched in my soul.

39. THE OLD MAN AND HIS DOG AUTHOR UNKNOWN

An old man and his dog were walking along a country road, enjoying the scenery, when it suddenly occurred to the man that he had died. He remembered dying, and realised, too, that the dog had been dead for many years.

He wondered where the road would lead them, and continued onward. After a while, they came to a high, white stone wall along one side of the road. It looked like fine marble.

At the top of a long hill, it was broken by a tall, white arch that gleamed in the sunlight. When he was standing before it, he saw a magnificent gate in the arch that looked like mother of pearl, and the street that led to the gate looked like pure gold. He was pleased that he had finally arrived at heaven, and the man and his dog walked toward the gate. As he got closer, he saw someone sitting at a beautifully carved desk off to one side. When he was close enough, he called out, "Excuse me, but is this heaven?" "Yes, it is, sir," the man answered. "Wow! Would you happen to have some water?" the man asked." Of course, sir. Come right in, and I'll have some ice water brought right up." The gatekeeper gestured to his rear, and the huge gate began to open. "I assume my friend can come in..." the man said, gesturing toward his dog. But the reply was, "I'm sorry, sir, but we don't accept pets." The man thought about it, then thanked the gatekeeper, turned back toward the road, and continued in the direction he had been going.

After another long walk, he reached the top of another long hill, and he came to a dirt road which led through a farm gate. There was no fence, and it looked as if the gate had never been closed, as grass had grown up around it. As he approached the gate, he saw a man just inside, sitting in the shade of a tree in a rickety old chair, reading a book. "Excuse me!" he called to the reader. "Do you have any water?" "Yeah, sure, there's a pump over there," the man said, pointing to a place that couldn't be seen from outside the gate. "Come on in and make yourself at home." "How about my friend here?" the traveler gestured to the dog. "He's welcome too, and there's a bowl by the pump," he said. They walked through the gate and, sure enough, there was an old-fashioned hand pump with a dipper hanging on it and a bowl next to it on the ground. The man filled the bowl for his dog, and then took a long drink himself. When both were satisfied, he and the dog walked back toward the man, who was sitting under the tree waiting for them, and asked, "What do you call this place?" the traveler asked. "This is heaven," was the answer. "Well, that's confusing," the traveler said. "It certainly doesn't look like heaven, and there's another man down the road who said that place was heaven." "Oh, you mean the place with the gold street and pearly gates?" "Yes, it was beautiful." "Nope. That's hell." "Doesn't it offend you for them to use the name of heaven like that?" "No. I can see how you might think so, but it actually saves us a lot of time. They screen out the people who are willing to leave their best friends behind."

Of course I didn't write that story, but it is true to say that I have been blessed to connected to our sprit animal friends.

It give me great joy to reunite the unconditional love a pet has for their human.

I am often greeted by dog, cats, budgies and horses from the spirit world. They come forward during public demonstrations and in private sittings.

Often people are surprised as to the why animals would be in heaven but I believe that the above story illustrates that perfectly. Why would't the fur babies in our physical life not be with us in our after life? Their love and loyalty being the purest that can be.

40. THE CARDIGAN

June 2017

I pulled the cream-cabled knitted cardigan around my shoulders and hugged the softness of the garment, oversized, homely and full of the essence of my Wise Owl Denise. The only physical thing I had of hers. When I learnt of her passing, I contacted her husband and asked if I should send it to him. She had been with me a few weeks before her death and left it behind in her hurry to catch the plane home. I was grateful he had said that I should keep it.

I use it often to feel her presence in times of great despair.

I can hear her soft sniffs, a habit she had in life, and at times her soft voice reassuring and encouraging me.

It has been just over a year now, but I still miss her as if it were yesterday. Unfortunately, I couldn't attend her funeral due to illness, and instead, I held a private service at my home. She was much loved by all who knew her.

Time is funny; you can leap into a moment in your head, a memory so vivid that clocks turn back and yesteryear can be found. I was blessed to have so many recollections of our antics.

I smiled and laughed at the memory of us both having uncontrollable giggles whilst attending a very serious Spiritual Sunday Church Service. We were sitting at the front, and the eyes of our tutors and the demonstrators were on us at Scarborough. We had been attending a course together there.

It took just one look with nothing said to create the notorious inappropriate giggles we were experiencing. It didn't go unnoticed with questions after the service about why we were so giddy. Unfortunately, we could not explain; Denise and I did not know why we experienced such joy.

I chuckled at the memory, which lifted my mood, which had been low. My uncle, who was like a second father to us, had passed. It was a sorrowful time.

Grief cares not about who you are, what you do, or if you are a medium. Grief has no timeline. It is not a year or two for most it is learning to live with the loss of a loved one.

Nestled in her cardigan, I felt her close. It is the cardigan I turn to in times of need. It gives me strength.

Objects you see hold the essence of those who wore them —a psychic imprint, something like a fingerprint, unique to the individual.

I pulled the cardigan closer like a hug and felt the courage to move forward to a day working with spirit in the knowledge that she would be with me, helping me to bring those exceptional connections close to those who sought my gift.

I gently removed the soft woollen garment and reverently hung it up in my closet for when I would need it next. I whispered Thank you, Denise, as I closed the wardrobe door.

Printed in Great Britain
by Amazon